REMEMBER...I AM WITH YOU

Remember... I AM With You

A MESSAGE FROM GOD

Rosa Díaz

PALMETTO
P U B L I S H I N G
Charleston, SC
www.PalmettoPublishing.com

Hardcover ISBN: 979-8-8229-2553-3
Paperback ISBN: 979-8-8229-2554-0
eBook ISBN: 979-8-8229-2555-7

ACKNOWLEDGMENTS

To Lesley and Paul, my gifts from heaven,

We cannot turn back time, nor can we rewrite our story. How I wish we could. What we can do, however, is take control of the remaining chapters. Throughout this process, I looked to you for motivation when I questioned whether I had anything valuable to share. I learned so many powerful lessons I wish I had known all along. These stand out the most, and I hope you find them helpful. Placing God first is ideal, but as you know, this was not always true for me. Thankfully, there is always a before and after in our lives; I can honestly say that if God is in the after, you will be just fine. Always look for the hidden blessings in the struggle, pain, and suffering. And remember to see life through God's lens; it is the only way to understand that it is a precious gift filled with limitless possibilities. And lastly, it is never too late to learn and practice the true meaning of forgiveness and unconditional love. I love you and am grateful to be your mom.

To Myles:

From the moment you were born, you became my inspiration for all good things. The first time I looked at you, I saw what unconditional love looks like. You are my ray of sunshine on cloudy days and my favorite person in the entire world. Remember that your superpower comes from being a child of the almighty God. Myles, you are the captain of my heart and my favorite superhero! I love you.

To my parents, family, and friends,

Mom, you are my example of positivity, perseverance, and resilience. You are also one of the kindest and most caring people I know. Thank you for making your family a priority. Dad, thank you for choosing me to be your daughter. I am grateful that you came into my life and for always loving and protecting me. Everyone should have such wonderful, loving, and supportive people. What a blessing you all are. Thank you for your patience, support, and incredible kindness, especially during my darkest times, and for being a part of my life journey. No connection was without purpose, and I am thankful you played a role in my growth; I would not be here without you. Whether it was long-term or momentary, I now understand that it was never about the length of time but about the lessons we must learn from one another. You can count on me, just as I have relied on you. May the Lord bless you all.

"In Loving Memory"

Angelica, you were the first one I read to, and I still remember how excited you were. I did it. I finished; you always believed in me. I wish you were still here to see and read the book. I know you would be so proud because you were proud then. I love you and miss you forever, my dear friend.

To Renee,

You are the messenger God chose to deliver the message. It all began with your obedient heart. At the time, we were both confused; we never imagined God's plan *was for those seven phrases to become a powerful healing reminder of His love and redemption. Thank you for listening to His voice. Your phone call that Saturday morning changed my life, and it is about to change many more. God bless you.*

Last but not least, to all those who remain trapped in a place that was supposed to be safe. Please know that you are not alone. This message offers hope and encourages you to take action. Let it serve as a guiding light to help you find answers and direction toward the healing path.

For I am the Lord your God who takes hold of your
right hand and says to you, do not fear; I will help you.

—Isaiah 41:13, NIV

We finally made it to our destination after a long journey. Ironically, I am at a loss for words to express my gratitude, but I will keep trying until my last breath. I find comfort in knowing that You already know how grateful I am. As the writing process unfolded, I hesitated to share my sinful life filled with countless mistakes. Still, I found solace knowing You paid the ransom at the cross for a sinner like me, and that is when I decided that nothing You ever ask of me is off limits. Thank you for showering me with your grace despite my imperfections. And for reminding me that I deserve forgiveness and unconditional love. I am humbled that You chose and inspired me to write this book. I give You all the credit because I am only the instrument that wrote the words. After all, You and I know who the real author is. Jesus, thank you for walking alongside me, not just through the process of writing this book but for my entire life. May Your Spirit, who inspired every word in this book, be felt by everyone searching for healing. I dedicate my life and this book to You, my one and all. It is time to share the path that leads back to You.

He heals the brokenhearted and
binds up their wounds.

– Psalm 147:3

Note from the author,

You are meant to be here—your presence is not a coincidence but a meaningful part of a greater plan. As you read these words, know that they are a message from God. Believe with certainty that we all have a unique role in His grand design. Writing this book took years of perseverance, but I always trusted God's perfect timing. Each chapter in this book addresses the five emotions that keep us from connecting with our Creator.

At the request of the Lord, I am sharing an unedited version of my story. Initially, I hesitated because I lacked courage and feared exposing the shameful events of my life. However, God reminded me that since the beginning of time, humans have struggled with admitting their mistakes and have always resorted to the practice of blame. God instructed Adam and Eve to avoid eating the fruit of a specific tree, but they were tempted and ate it. As a result of their actions, they became aware of their nakedness. Trying to hide their disobedience, they sewed fig leaves together to cover themselves. Even though God knew what had occurred in the garden, He allowed Adam to confess his disobedience and take responsibility for his actions. Instead, Adam blamed God. And Eve then blamed the serpent for deceiving her.

From this moment on, we inherited the practice of blaming others, producing the same result: our disconnection from God. In this message, God reminds us of His grace and invites us to approach Him exposing our sinful, and imperfect human state. Our Creator has given us free will, and He patiently waits for us to return to Him. He plans to heal what we have been hiding.

Remember that your flaws are known to the Lord, and perfection belongs to Him alone. Your story is unique, and your challenges, struggles, and pain are real. You are a child of the almighty God worthy of love and forgiveness. Do not let anyone tell you otherwise. We are all broken and must be restored. Salvation is a gift within reach. You are saved by grace; Jesus paid the price. However, to receive the ultimate gift, you must choose to return home. It is time to remove the fig leaves, take responsibility for your actions, and reconnect with your Creator. May these words inspire you to trust in God's plan and to live a life of purpose and fulfillment.

CONTENTS

Introduction

Have you ever wondered how obedient you would be if God asked you to do something for Him? If your answer is no, neither had I. Since I was a young girl, I believed in God and sensed He was always nearby. As a teenager, I was walking home one day, and a stranger approached me and handed me a flyer with images and scriptures warning me about the "end-times." I became intrigued and started believing that "heaven and hell" were actual destinations. What I remember about the flyer is that it portrayed God sitting on His throne, waiting to pass judgment. Seeing that image frightened me, and I became convinced that although He loved me, He would be harsh on judgment day. I knew that I would eventually have to answer for my bad choices and behavior. As time passed, my belief that He was always near never ceased. I had a sense of peace and confidence because I chose to believe in God. I have always tried to do what is right. All I wanted was to live a life that pleased Him.

A few years ago, I learned there is a difference between choosing and being chosen. God planned to show me the difference one Saturday morning when I received an unexpected call from a friend I had not seen or spoken to in over three years; I could never anticipate what would happen. She kindly asked if she could come over for a visit. I replied, "Of course." She said, "I am on my way." All I could say was, "Sounds great! See you soon." I have always enjoyed having company; however, I like to prepare before their arrival. I ensure the house is in order, the candles are lit, disbursing an inviting scent, and the cake stand on my kitchen island contains a homemade pastry. So I was shocked when I quickly agreed. Maybe because she did not give me a choice. She lived about an hour away, and that much time had passed when our doorbell rang. My family was home. We were all excited to see her. After greeting her, they left.

Once we were alone, we had some small talk, and she said, "I am sure you are surprised I called." I told her I was delighted to see her but was also curious about the urgency since she showed up within an hour. We sat in the family room, and she said, "I know this may sound strange, but I am here because God has sent me to deliver a message for you. Do you believe me?"

"Yes, I do," I replied. But deep inside, I was skeptical. I did not confess this to her since she had driven an hour to see me.

She mentioned that God had made the same request in April of that year, but she ignored Him; by now, it was September. She said, "I have been awake since 4:00 a.m., and once again, the Lord has been asking me to come and see you;

I wrestled with His petition because, clearly, I was uncertain what I would say to you. But I decided to obey His request. I began driving, and as He gave me your message, I would pull over to write it down. All I had was this notepad from a hotel." She showed me the note; it consisted of seven phrases. "I am not sure if this means anything to you, but I wrote it down word for word." She prayed, and I instantly felt the undeniable presence of the Lord.

After reading the first phrase, she asked me if it made any sense. I told her that I needed to strengthen my connection with God; this might be a reminder. She continued, and upon hearing the second phrase, there was no doubt God was speaking to me. She finished reading the rest of the message and handed me the three pieces of paper containing what I now believed was a message from God. I was in tears, and I had so many questions, but she said, "I am sorry, I have nothing else to share with you. All He asked is that I deliver it today." I thanked her, and we said goodbye.

I was stunned and confused. I called my sister to share what had happened; she asked me, "Can you believe how special you are that God took the time to send you a written message?" I remember always feeling special and believing that I have a specific purpose to fulfill. And now I know this is true for all of us.

However, feeling special had become a distant memory at this point in my life. As I held the note containing these seven phrases, I knew my sister was right because I did feel special receiving a message from God. Sitting there alone and feeling incredibly emotional, I asked Him, why me? Discovering the reason and its meaning became an unanswered question for seven years. If I am honest, my life did not turn out as I had hoped or dreamed it would; come to think of it, it is common for our lives to turn out differently. After spending thirty-five years with my partner, I am now alone. We began dating when we were just fifteen years old. Despite how young and immature we were, somehow, we developed a strong bond. It was not the healthiest of relationships, but it was all I knew. Like all couples, we shared happy moments and lived through many challenging times throughout the years.

I experienced depression and anxiety. I am not proud to say this, but several times, I contemplated suicide. Even though our relationship was where I learned many difficult lessons, it was tough to accept when it fell apart. I lived with so much regret. These emotions deleted my sense of worthiness. I often attempted to connect with God but could no longer feel His presence as I became convinced that I had disappointed Him and that He had also abandoned me. I felt broken, beyond repair. The night I recall as the darkest of nights, I decided to call on God one last time. It was the wisest decision since the overwhelming pain had deleted my desire to live. I am ashamed to admit it, but I planned to end my life that night. As I struggled to find a reason to go on, I recalled that since I was a child, I was certain there was a specific reason God created me. Feeling lost and hopeless, I cried out to Him, pleading with Him to help and save me. I said, "Jesus, I know You have a specific purpose for my life, and I need You to show me because I have not figured it out, and I do not want to die before I accomplish what You brought me here to do." I remember praying with all my heart and soul; I did not expect a response as soon as I got it. It was time for God to reveal the meaning of the first phrase.

The following day, I went for a walk, and the thought "write a book" just came to me as an idea. Thinking it was strange, I continued walking but started seeing the words. They were in cursive and lowercase. As the day went on, the image did not cease. Once again, I called my sister. I told her what was happening, and she asked me, "Has it ever occurred to you to write a book?"

I burst out in laughter and said, "No! Are you kidding? I hardly even like to read; why would writing a book ever cross my mind?"

Then she said, "Well, if you asked the Lord to reveal your purpose, maybe this is part of it. Keep praying."

I began to see a therapist in Mexico and would travel once a week to meet her. While driving there the next day, I was now annoyed because I could see the message as a banner across a television screen announcing, "Breaking news." I told God, "Even if I could write a book, what do You want me to write? Why would You ask me to write a book?" A few minutes passed, and I perceived seven chapters and thought it sounded like a short book. In that instant, I remembered the note He sent me had seven phrases. I was excited because it finally started to make sense; I believed it would be easy to write this book. Little did I know, I was in for a shocking surprise! When I returned home, I immediately picked up my note. I read it over and over. Each phrase left me with more questions than answers. I told Him, "This is not making any sense," but as I came to find out, God also planned to teach me something I lacked: patience and the true meaning of having faith.

Writing a book was something I had never considered. Therefore, I must disclose that before receiving this message and request, the extent of my writing was at most a couple of phrases on a greeting card. The last thing I would ever sign up for is to reveal personal and shameful experiences. I also did not want to walk down memory lane and relive my past, but it was part of God's plan; He wanted me to reflect on all I had lived. This process took me to dark places and brought to light memories of experiences I had buried so deep. I must allow the not-so-fond memories to resurface. The truth is that even with my belief in God and trying to do the right thing, I made so many mistakes, and failure was the result. My story did not have a "happily ever after" ending. The overwhelming pain and guilt over the loss of my relationship weighed heavily.

As I began dissecting so many life-altering experiences, all intended to reveal lessons I needed to learn; I could not avoid the shame and disappointment I felt. I recalled the questions I asked myself many years ago. Why did I disconnect from God? Why have I betrayed myself? Can I compensate for the pain and worry I caused my loved ones? That is when I realized the message in my note contains God's purpose for my life. It was time to learn why He sent the message, its meaning, and the reason for choosing me. Seven years ago, God knew I would soon plead for Him to rescue me. His plan was for me to refer to the note and discover the powerful message so that I may find my way back to Him. It is time to surrender. The Lord is about to reveal the meaning of unconditional love. That September, God took the time to send me a beautiful reminder that He has never forgotten me; He said, "Remember, I AM With You."

CHAPTER 1

Belong

You have forgotten where you came from.

*Fear not, for I have redeemed you; I have
called you by name; You are mine.*

—Isaiah 43:1 NKJV

I received my message at a time when "apparently" all was
great. But I realized that I habitually placed God on the back
burner when things were going well and I had everything I
needed. Unfortunately, this is a common truth for many of us.
My partner and I started our life together with hope, dreams,
and determination to achieve our goals. We began by renting
an apartment, purchasing a small house, and eventually buy-
ing our dream home. Most of us relate "success" with material
possessions; I now know this is an inaccurate perception. Our
family lived in our beautiful home with our two wonderful,
healthy children, and we both had thriving businesses. It appeared we had arrived at the intersection of success. We were
finally reaping the benefits after pouring ourselves into hard
work and many years of sacrifice and dedication. At last, we
met the criteria for a successful life. Except no one ever knows
what goes on behind closed doors.

As a young girl, I spent countless hours drawing my dream
house. As an adult, I realized that some areas of my life had

exceeded my childhood dreams, and in others, I lived experiences I could have never imagined. There are two things I have never doubted: God exists, and I am blessed. My mother was raised Catholic but explored different denominations. All of them claimed to be "the chosen one." I remember telling God at that young age that I was confused. I did not know which one to choose. All I wanted was to be with Him when I died. In hindsight, my awareness of God spiked my interest in His teachings. Even though I am not religious, I always connected with Him and felt protected. That has not changed to this day, as He is the one with whom I speak daily. Lately, more often than before, especially at night, when I cannot sleep because He wakes me up to write. I know that God is all I need because, without a doubt, I believe He is the way, the truth, and the life, as stated in the Bible.

I was born in Agua Prieta, Sonora, on the border with Douglas, Arizona. My parents married after and because of my birth. My sister was born a year and a half later. They divorced when I was three years old. After the divorce, my father was not a part of our lives, and I always referred to him by his first name. My grandfather lived with us, and we were close to him. It was a blessing because he was like a father to me until he passed away when I was eighteen, which was a significant loss for me. My mom remarried a couple of years later. Even though I was initially jealous that my stepdad was receiving her attention, I eventually came to appreciate him. They had two sons, and this completed our family. I had a very humble upbringing. We lived in a small house with the bare necessities, simple furnishings, nothing fancy. My parents worked hard to provide the comforts of home. We always had everything we needed and occasionally some things we wanted.

During those years, I was often rebellious and angry, which stands out when I reflect on that time. I did not always show respect toward my mother, and we would often argue. I have a strong and stubborn personality, always ready for a debate, and those close to me say that these traits persist to this day. Regrettably, I took out my frustration on my mother. It was only recently that I realized how much my parents' divorce affected me. I may have unconsciously blamed my mother for my father's absence, as it was easier than facing the fact that my dad decided not to be a part of my life. I know now that relationships end for numerous reasons, and I was not very considerate toward my mother.

Other than that, my childhood was quite normal. I was an average kid who often argued with my siblings and sneaked money to buy candy. From an early age I had a sense of responsibility and knew that my actions would have consequences. I became overly cautious about what I did, though I was only sometimes mindful of my words. Despite that, I developed a lot of self-control with what I believed were more severe offenses than the ones mentioned above. My father hardly showed any interest after their divorce. He married a couple more times, and I also have three brothers and a younger sister from those marriages. Although my stepfather, whom I refer to as Dad, is a blessing, his commitment to my sister and me made it even more challenging to excuse my father's detachment. I struggled to understand how a perfect stranger who entered my life was willing to assume responsibility and step into the role my biological father never intended to fulfill.

Growing up without the love of a biological father can profoundly impact a child, with the effects not always immediately apparent. I experienced a range of emotions, including anger, fear of abandonment, insecurity, and low self-confidence, all of which have persisted throughout my life. I exhibited codependency traits, constantly seeking acceptance and approval from others while putting their needs ahead of mine. However, I was determined to act responsibly and never used my father's absence as an excuse for misbehaving. My ultimate wish was that if my father ever became interested in me, he would see that I was a good person and want to establish a relationship. To that end, I worked hard in school, always sat in the front of the class to avoid trouble, and consistently achieved straight As.

Additionally, I helped care for my siblings and grandfather at home. Despite all my efforts, however, there were no signs that my father was interested in establishing a relationship with me. As a result, I began to feel angry and resentful. Our family moved to Chandler, Arizona, during my third grade in elementary. We faced numerous challenges, ranging from living there illegally to the language barrier; it was a feeling that lacked a sense of belonging. My siblings and I were bullied for not having nice clothes and not knowing the language. It was challenging to go from being at the top of the class to sitting in a classroom with no idea what anyone was saying.

I found comfort in math since, in Mexico, they began teaching advanced math in an earlier grade; I excelled in this subject. Over time, I became fluent in English and received multiple awards for my academic performance. Unfortunately, my stepfather lost his job at the farming company, and we would soon move again. I always wanted to return to Mexico; it was home. Ever since we moved to the States, I felt like an intruder; I wanted to return to where I knew I belonged. After my father lost his job, he struggled to find another job. I have known since then how difficult it is for undocumented workers. My parents wanted more opportunities for us and were still determining if we would stay in the States.

In the meantime, they found a job cleaning yards. I knew they were struggling financially, and I begged them to get me a job to help them. It was easy back then—they just wanted someone to get the work done. They hired me; I was only twelve. We were working in scorching weather. One day I became dizzy and almost fainted; I was dehydrated. My sister took my place the next day while I stayed home to recover. The next-door neighbor was friends with my parents, and since he had no home phone, he frequently received calls at our house. That morning there was a call for our neighbor; I informed him and continued with my chores while he took the call. Once he hung up, he lit a cigarette and began making conversation. While standing there, I felt dizzy and lost my balance; he quickly got up to assist me, asking what was wrong. I explained why I was home that day, and he asked for rubbing alcohol. I walked toward the bathroom but felt uneasy as he followed me. I returned to the living room, and he poured rubbing alcohol on his hands for me to smell. Then he rubbed the back of my neck and tried to slide his hand down my blouse as he tried to kiss me. I was terrified. To this day, I have no idea how, but I was able to push him so hard that he landed in the corner of the room.

I cannot explain where I got the strength, but I know there was divine intervention. God was protecting me. Once my parents came home from work and found out what had happened, they were distraught. My dad was so mad he went next door to look for him, but the coward had fled and never returned to his house. We never saw him again. My parents asked me what I wanted to do, and I told them we should move back to Mexico. They did not call the police; they were scared of getting in trouble since we lived there illegally. Within a couple of weeks, we were back in Mexico. When we moved to the States, my grandfather had stayed, and I was sad because he was all alone. I missed him so much; I was relieved to be home. As soon as we arrived, it was clear it would be challenging for us.

We had a lot of work to catch up on regarding school. At the same time, my parents struggled to make ends meet. I felt so guilty. They never blamed me, but I blamed myself because I thought I had done something wrong that provoked the incident. All I wanted to do was forget about it. I became overly cautious and started to question people's intentions.

After our return to Mexico, my father began making attempts to see my sister and me. It seemed like he had a change of heart. He would come around our school every day, hoping to speak with us. We were not interested in seeing him. I remember he drove an old brown Chevy truck, which made it easy to avoid him. We would hide until we believed it was safe not to run into him. Then, one day he must have figured out that we were trying to avoid him, so he remained out of sight until he saw us. He said he wanted to get to know us and buy us whatever we needed. My sister was a bit more forgiving. I, on the other hand, was not interested. I turned him away and told him that our stepfather had always taken care of us and that he should not bother since he had not been in touch for years. I was hurt and angry that he was ignorant of the fact that all I needed was for him to issue an apology and tell me that he cared and loved me. I was not impressed by his attempts to buy my affection. Despite being hurt and disappointed that my father abandoned me, I remained committed to my values and stayed out of trouble.

As a teenager, I was very naive and calm. I enjoyed being home with my siblings and playing with my dolls. One
Saturday morning we went to visit our cousins across the border in Douglas. After hanging out for a while, they showed me
a yearbook and told me to look at the cute boys, but I was not
interested. Later in the day, I walked into the bedroom and
opened the yearbook that was left on the bed. My eyes focused
on a cute boy with adorable dimples. I asked my cousin about
him, and she said he was in high school with my older cousin.
Unbeknownst to me, she proceeded to tell him I thought he
was cute. He asked her for a picture of me, and once he saw
me, he thought I was pretty and wanted to meet me. By the
time we met, I already had a crush on a boy at school and was
no longer interested in him. But a few months later, we ran
into each other again, and he asked me for my phone number.
We would talk every night, sometimes for hours on end. Then,
in the fall of 1984, he asked me if I wanted to be his girlfriend.
I was surprised how that simple question had the power to
give me a sense of belonging.

He was my first boyfriend. I had crushes before but never
anything this formal. He went out of his way to make me feel
special. He was very thoughtful, sent me flowers, and wrote
beautiful cards. Although he was busy with school, sports, and
work, he always made time for me and took me on dates. My
mom knew his family, and she approved of us dating. Everyone
in my family liked him, and once I met his family, they also

accepted and liked me. My feelings for him grew, and I became convinced he was "the one." Remember your first love? The one that fills you with hope that you can survive anything together? He was that for me, even though we were just a couple of innocent kids. There are times I wish we had met later in life, and I often wonder if things would have turned out differently if we had. But I have learned that everything happens when and how it is supposed to.

From the start, our immaturity and inexperience contributed to our unhealthy relationship. He was jealous and expressed his opinion on what I should wear when we went out. He would ask me to wait for him instead of going with my friends. At that age, this behavior was complimentary. I thought he was proud and wanted to spend time with me instead of realizing it was about control. He was my first; I believed I had more to lose if we did not stay together. Those days, it was customary for our mothers to teach us that if we lost our virginity, no other man would want to marry us. This way of thinking was one reason I would later settle in the relationship. But more importantly, I knew I had disappointed God, felt terrible guilt, and was determined to make things work.

We were quite different. He enjoyed going out and liked to drink and party every weekend, but I did not. Despite all our differences, we cared for and loved each other. I began feeling pressured to change and become more outgoing, but thankfully I stayed true to my convictions and beliefs. Although I did notice a change, I developed a strong attachment and became very jealous and possessive, just as he was toward me. Then there were rumors that he was seeing other girls. I caught him once. I felt more insecure about our relationship and myself. The feeling of rejection introduced by my father was present once again, making me question if I was not enough and if something was wrong with me.

We became overly attached; we would break up, but soon we were back together. We could not be apart. Somehow, he always managed to convince me to give it another try. It was difficult not to take him back. He is very friendly, intelligent, charming, and incredibly talented. I was so attracted to him. He was also a hard worker and always a great provider. Despite the fact that we had few things in common, for some time, our values aligned since we had similar backgrounds. He always admired that I was conservative, and although he did not enjoy being home, he liked that I was content with spending time quietly at home. I remained committed to him. After our first intimate encounter, I knew that I would be loyal no matter what.

In January 1989, we discovered we were expecting our first child. Despite being only twenty years old, we were happy and excited to become parents. The great news of our pregnancy provided much-needed hope that this would motivate him to make better choices. As I focused on the baby's arrival, I did not notice that his casual drug use, which he always denied, had become a severe problem. I had no idea what to look for since I never used drugs; naturally, it was unlikely that I would recognize the symptoms.

The birth of our daughter was such a happy time; she was the first grandchild for both sides of the family. Parenthood provided a distraction from our problems. He was excited and became a wonderful father. I was grateful my daughter would experience what I never had; she would have a loving and supportive father. Becoming a parent reinforced my belief not to give up and to remain focused on what I had always desired, a home and a family. When our daughter turned two, we received more good news—we were once again expecting. I wanted a son because our daughter was quite a daddy's girl. My wish came true; we had our son.

There were signs that my partner's drug use was out of control and he needed intervention. A few months after the birth of our son, he got in trouble and entered a court-ordered rehabilitation center. I was faithfully by his side and was more committed than ever because of our children. Understanding substance abuse was challenging for me. I believed abstaining from unhealthy habits was as easy as saying no. I naively intended to help him and thought I could positively influence him to change. The rehab center provided family counseling; it was a requirement. It became an excellent opportunity to discuss and work on our problems. I finally understood the cycle of drug abuse, how it works, and how I contributed. Attending counseling is where I first heard and learned the word "enabler," which I unknowingly had become.

We received much-needed insight and direction. I constantly reminded him of his potential, qualities, and strengths, hoping he would see the value of adopting a healthier lifestyle. I did not know then, but I was turning him into my life project. After completing his stay in the rehab center, most of his so-called friends left him once he gained a sober outlook on life. It was a blessing for him, an opportunity for a fresh start. It appeared he was a changed man. He reconnected with his faith and committed his life to God. We lost everything we had, but to me, it did not matter. I focused on a new beginning.

We had several years where things were great. We started going to church, and he continued to practice his twelve steps. I welcomed the healthy, sober man he had become. It all indicated that the tough times were behind us. However, it would not last long. The reality was that most of our years together were like a roller-coaster ride. There were many happy times, and it was when I held on tighter to my dream of having a family and a home. We purchased a small house on the outskirts of town and enjoyed a peaceful quiet life away from the city. Those were our happiest years; he and our kids would agree.

Just like during the good times, when things were great, the same applied to the tough times; they were awful. I learned many lessons over the span of our relationship. These two I should have paid closer attention to early on. The first one is that despite having the best intentions to influence or encourage someone to change, the decision to change is optional; it is only up to the individual to realize they need to improve or adjust how they carry on. No one changes until they choose to. I desperately wanted him to see his potential and make better choices; he was not ready to change, even if it would improve his life. The second lesson is that I must be my priority. Loving and caring for myself consciously and intentionally first is not selfish but a healthy practice. In trying to keep my family together, I forgot I mattered too. I focused on everyone else's needs, preventing me from dealing with all the emotions destroying me. It was a costly mistake. Everything that happens has a purpose; even if, at that moment, I could not discern it, all experiences in time reveal valuable lessons.

Looking back, what do a couple of inexperienced fifteen-year-olds know or understand about relationships, loyalty, or love? Relationships are serious commitments where we assume many responsibilities and live through significant, life-altering experiences. Although we later appreciate the lessons that stem from making wrong choices, the consequences often take time to present themselves. Over the years, there were signs I should move in a different direction. It seemed as if God whispered, suggesting I needed to let go. I would unexpectedly run into the note and read it, but it did not make sense, and I wondered why God had sent it to me. I am more ashamed than ever. Holding the note had me questioning if I was indeed the right recipient. Unknowingly, my entire life would soon shatter, making it impossible for me to try yet another unsuccessful attempt to put it back together.

I vividly remember that toward the end, on our way home after visiting family, I sat utterly silent. In the past, during our travels, I would talk nonstop all the way home; sitting there speechless was unusual. By now, I had grown tired of talking without him engaging. As I looked out the window with a blank stare, he turned and asked, "What are you thinking about?"

I replied with a question I had asked myself as a young girl shortly after becoming aware of God's presence. "Do you believe that God created us with a specific purpose?"

He replied, "I believe the main reason is to live life to the fullest." I thought about his answer, and I realized how unhappy I was. I was not living the life I had dreamed of, and more importantly, a life that pleased God.

Not long after that, we parted ways. While I lost myself in the relationship, the ending cleared the path to focus on finding myself—although at the time, I could not see or appreciate it because of all the pain and despair. Sadly, I know many people who have lost their partners after a divorce or break up, including my mom. All of them have stated that it is next to losing a loved one through death, the most agonizing experience one will go through. All the stories had one thing in

common: regret over focusing on and prioritizing their partner or spouse while forgetting about themselves. I would have
to agree. The pain introduced after losing my lifelong partner
was unbearable. I am unsure if my abysmal pain relates to the
number of years invested; truthfully, all I wanted was to die.

I could not handle the pain, nor did I want to. Nothing
made sense; this type of loss is heartbreaking. It was then that
I perceived a new kind of fear. This time, it was about surviving
on my own. It began to invade and suffocate me. I felt lost. I
had to remind myself to breathe even though that was the last
thing I wanted to do. One would think that ending a relationship would be easy to accept for someone who had lived and
contributed to such a toxic environment. Even though it was
long overdue, the pain was unmanageable.

At last, it is time to let God know I am ready to shift my
focus back to Him. Remember I mentioned placing God on
the back burner because "all was great"? I became aware that
there are times when blessings disguise and bury themselves in
our suffering. Amid the pain, I shifted the focus toward Him
with one question: What now? God knows I made choices
that led me down this dead-end road, but ultimately it led me
back to Him. He kindly reminded me of the young girl who
knew He was near no matter where she was, of our conversations and how much He enjoyed them. I knew then He loved
me and that I belonged. Over time, our connection dissipated.
My reaction to life's overwhelming events filled me with guilt

and shame, and just like that, I let it happen; I disconnected from God and stopped listening to His voice, and eventually, I let go. I tried to reconnect many times, but the shame of what my life had become prevented me from further attempts. Like clockwork, when all else fails, look up.

Everything was now more uncertain than ever. Do you remember me? I asked Him as I was kneeling beside my bed. I was crying and pleading with Him to take away this pain because it was preventing me from finding a reason to live. I told Him I no longer had an identity and did not belong anywhere. "I am completely lost and ashamed of the life I forged so far from You, ignoring all your warnings and whispers." As I knelt there crying and begging Him to help me, I suddenly wanted to reach for my note, which He so kindly sent me years ago. It was inside a devotional book on my nightstand. Holding the note with the message that never made sense, I got back on my knees and read, "You have forgotten where you came from." This is the first phrase, His first loving reminder. At that precise moment, the Lord revealed the meaning of the phrase I had read multiple times before without the ability to understand it. He was asking me, "Why do you believe you no longer have an identity? Why do you feel like you do not belong? Your identity is that you are a child of the almighty God and Creator of the universe—you belong to Me. You are mine. I have been waiting to take you into my arms, heal and restore you and remind you that you are loved unconditionally." In that instant, I saw God's hand upon my life. He was always with me, patiently waiting for my return, to comfort and love me without judgment. It was the darkest of nights, yet I found a glimpse of hope.

Loss is devastating and heartbreaking; it brought pain and left a void I never imagined existed. Yet experiencing loss and failure brought a new direction and perspective. I know first-hand what happens when the things and people I was attached to are no longer the primary focus of my life. After the strong attachments were lost and broken, I finally shifted my focus toward my Creator. The revelation within this phrase has reinforced my faith and reconnected me with God, the only trustworthy source. Even though I felt rejected and unworthy, He lovingly and graciously came to calm my soul that night. He filled my longing to belong by reminding me that He chose me long ago and that I am worthy and loved. He wants me to remember that I am here with purpose and intention. When I encounter moments of fear and doubt about whether I belong, I have the answer and confidence in knowing I am a child of the almighty God.

Note to the Reader: Remember...You Belong

There were many times when I felt an immeasurable empti-ness; it derived from the revoked feeling of belonging. A time will come when we perceive a void within us because we will undoubtedly experience rejection, abandonment, and loss. It is painful and terrifying to lose people we love and the life we used to live; I know because it happened to me. The irony is that we perceive the importance of belonging after encounter-ing rejection, failure, and loss. We cannot avoid experiencing loss; it is a predictable part of life, as in losing a loved one, a relationship, or a job. The reason you have lost your sense of belonging may be different from mine, but I believe we all arrive at the same crossroads, asking whether or where we be-long. When we find the courage, we begin our search for the answer, which leads us to the path that connects us to the only source of belonging that truly matters, which is God. For me, it has been the most significant of blessings. If you find your-self at this intersection, do not fear; this means you are closer to discovering that God chose you long ago and, therefore, you have always belonged. The phrase for this chapter is the most powerful phrase of the whole message because recalling and connecting to whom we belong is the foundation to begin healing and discovering our worth. Only God, our Creator, can fill this void. Be at peace; you belong.

CHAPTER 2

Courage

You live in fear every day of your life.
That is where your anger comes from.

Be strong and courageous.

—Joshua 1:9, NKJV

Some experiences require God's divine intervention to ensure we understand them. I lived in a destructive cycle most of my life, unaware of its seriousness. That is until I received the message. Every time I read this phrase, I knew it connected to an incident from early on in our relationship, which forever changed me. I immediately suppressed it and, therefore, never dealt with the trauma brought on by the experience.

I have heard the expression that our lives can change instantly and without warning; this is true for me because of what happened that night. As a child, I was afraid of many things but overcame most as I grew older. However, I discovered a new type of fear later in life, which I was fortunate not to know about until that day. Unfortunately, that fear became all too familiar from that day forward. I wish I could say that this fear was unique to me; the sad truth is that it is all too common in our world.

My encounter with this fear was through an unexpected and violent act at the hands of the person I loved. Nothing could prepare me for how I would react during and following that event. The truth is that trying to excuse his actions because he was high on drugs when it took place did not lessen the effect and the damage it caused. Shortly after it occurred, it was as if I had entered into a contract with fear. From that day forward, this fear owned me, controlled me, and altered my identity and how I lived. A perfect way to describe it is that it turned me into its prisoner. It changed the possibility of becoming who I was supposed to be.

I felt safe and confident in making decisions before the incident. However, soon after, those privileges would be something I no longer enjoyed. Making a simple decision scared me; the struggle with doubt and hesitation began, and I became even more insecure. Believing I was no longer safe with the man I loved would be what transformed me into the outraged person I became. Ironically, I did not understand what was happening to me and why I was always so angry. Although the target for most of my anger was the person who had caused me harm, I still felt extreme guilt for reacting that way.

Sadly, he would not remain my only target for long, as the anger reached the innocent people in my life. The fear brought on the rage, and since I never understood the connection, I did not know how to stop the adverse reactions. After releasing the anger and witnessing how it hurt those closest to me, I was highly disappointed in myself, which intensified my anger. I became trapped.

The power of deliverance within this phrase does not cease to amaze me. I know God sent this phrase to help me understand how closely related fear and anger are. After the event on that fateful night, I suppressed the memory. If I intend to heal, I must remember all the unpleasant moments I buried to avoid addressing them. There is power in the word "remember" because what set me free is found through recalling all I have lived through and survived. When I began to write about this topic, it was challenging for two reasons: the stigma associated with domestic violence and the fact that it required me to expose something I had no intention of sharing. Honestly, admitting I stayed as long as I did in an abusive environment and became an active participant in it is incredibly shameful.

Although most know that domestic violence exists, you may not be aware that someone within your circle of family, friends, and acquaintances has lived or may currently be involved in this type of relationship. It is unlikely you will hear about it because it is not something a person wants to talk about openly if they lived through it, or are currently living it. You may only find out until there is an arrest or death in connection to it. Domestic violence is complex, and more so is understanding those involved, especially the "victim." Countless articles, books, and documentaries address this topic and its patterns with the intent of spreading awareness, but truthfully, it is unlikely that you will be able to relate with someone who has been mistreated. Because frankly, if you have never been manipulated, threatened, hurt, or about to lose your life in the hands of the person you love, you cannot comprehend the magnitude of the fear one faces.

Overcoming violence is even more challenging when one has a family and multiple ties to the alleged perpetrator. Abuse is not always obvious either; there are variables and levels of abuse, and not all produce visible proof. Therefore, one might believe the relationship does not qualify as abusive without violence. Unfortunately, there are too many forms of abuse; some of the most common are physical, emotional, financial, and sexual. An important note is that just because the abuse may not be violent and leave physical evidence, that does not mean there aren't damaging side effects. While there are countless emotions, fear is the leading character in all the stories.

Once it was clear I could not avoid writing about my experience, I viewed this as an opportunity to learn more about fear. I searched for "things people are afraid of," and these are just a few examples: thunderstorms, death, lightning, snakes, heights, flying, darkness, failure, public speaking, etc. I must admit that some of these things are also on my list. Yet fearing the person you love, the one you may have a family with, was not on that list. So obviously, neither are suggestions on ways to overcome this fear. I hope my story helps you understand that living this way is challenging and that leaving a relationship is not always as easy as it appears. It is time to remove the mask I have worn for an entire lifetime—the one that gave me an excuse to cover up my reality. If I expect to free myself from this fear, I need to expose the whole truth, the one I tried so desperately to hide, the same one that so many others live with and are fearfully and shamefully hiding behind.

There are many moments in my life I wish would have an alternative course or end, like in the movies; this is one of those times. The night it occurred was an ordinary evening. Dinner was ready. My daughter and I were waiting for him to come home; he took longer than usual, and she fell asleep. I do not recall when it occurred, but I know I was not yet twenty-two years old; it was around 7:00 p.m. and getting dark. He finally arrived but was acting a bit strange. Shortly after, without warning, I had a loaded gun to my head. One of the definitions of fear is "an unpleasant, often strong emotion caused by anticipation or awareness of danger." Sounds accurate.

On this day, I found out fear has several levels. At first, my intuition warned me something was wrong. He walked in, talking to himself. I could not understand what he said, so I asked, "Did you say something?" but he did not answer. He walked to the bedroom, and I could still hear him speaking to himself. "Dinner is ready. Are you hungry?" I asked. He returned to the living room, where my daughter and I were, closed all the blinds, and locked the door. I asked, "Is something wrong?" And he mumbled no. I knew something was wrong; this is when fear manifested itself. I began to feel nervous and a bit scared. He headed down the hallway to our bedroom again, and I heard a gun click. In that instant, fear found a new home.

The next thing I remember is that man I loved, the one I wanted to spend the rest of my life with, grabbed me by my hair, and with his hand shaking, pointed a loaded gun to my head as he began screaming that he would kill me and then kill himself. And this was when fear reached its next level, turning into terror. It was all surreal, as if I were watching a scene from a movie. I could see my beautiful little girl asleep a few feet away, and I just wanted to hold her because I feared it could be the last time. He informed me he had no intention of hurting her. After hearing this, I tried to remain calm and talk to him; I told him I did not understand what was happening, but I knew he had a plan. He accused me of cheating over a two-minute phone call that appeared on the cell phone bill, a call he had asked me to make to a friend of his I barely knew. Calmly, I reminded him that he asked me to call his friend and relay a message on his behalf. He was paranoid; his drug problem was clearly out of control. In the turmoil of what was happening, I smelled gasoline and saw a red container in the kitchen. I started to panic because it appeared we would all die.

That night, that event changed my life forever. It completely distorted how I have lived and, sadly, how I love. No one intervened after this gun incident; they wrote it off as a "couple quarrel." I am not blaming anyone, but this being the first violent encounter, I thought I might be exaggerating, and it was not as bad as I thought since no one reacted to the incident. Afterward, I tried to forget what happened because the fact that I loved this man was still my reality. Instead of thinking about my daughter's and my safety, something happened, and somehow, I shifted the focus toward him; I wanted to help him. Unknowingly, I became familiar with the terms "enabler" and "codependent." All I could think about was finally having what I desired: a home and a family. And I was not ready to give that up. I convinced myself he would never have put us in harm's way if it were not for his drug problem since, up to this incident, there had never existed an indication that something of this magnitude would happen. I believed that once he got help, everything would be normal again.

My biggest mistake was making the first excuse on his behalf. All possibilities of a life with love and respect and my sense of worth ceased from that day forward. Unfortunately, the first excuse would lead to hundreds more. I now understand that it was on that day the codependency that manifested as a result of my father's absence when I was a child took over. The most common question everyone has when one remains in an abusive relationship is: Why do we stay? In my case, I began my relationship with fear through that violent and cowardly act, but it took on a life of its own over the years. It erased my self-confidence and the courage I knew I had. It also erased my dreams, passion, and hope; worst of all, I stopped believing in my self-worth. Fear invaded my life like I had a disability.

Once it appeared, it never left, and neither did I; I was too scared to walk away. The few times I would find a small ounce of courage to leave him, I would feel guilty because once he fell deep into his drug habit, all his friends abandoned him, and I could not walk away when he needed me the most. It was so difficult to make sense of what was right and wrong. It is not an excuse, but I was so young there was no possible way to have handled things differently.

Nothing ever made sense after that day. Fear and anger became my faithful companions. All I wanted was to return to the moment before my life got so messy. There were many years after the first encounter when nothing like that happened. I cannot recall when, how, or why the violence and threats began again. However, the damage was done. The environment in our home was far from peaceful and safe. Disrespect and abuse became a staple. While I lived at home with my parents, we heard them disagree and fight, but we never witnessed violence. I never knew such toxic and dangerous relationships existed or I would live in one.

I was so disappointed in myself. Before the incident, I was confident and intelligent, with a bright future ahead of me, but all I knew now was fear and anger. As time passed, guilt, shame, and regret appeared. I was so embarrassed to remain in such a toxic and dangerous relationship. My life became about justifying the behavior and making excuses for him; I blamed myself and attempted to dilute the intensity of the violence and deny my reality. I kept hoping things would get better. Instead, the more I tried, and the worse things got, I became angrier and more frustrated, and I desperately tried to bury each encounter to avoid facing the end. One of my biggest regrets is that it never occurred to me to consider or assess the damage it was causing our children. I became trapped in this toxic cycle; I wanted the fights and the abuse to stop, but I did not want to lose him, our family, or our home. I began isolating myself once I learned that others noticed something was wrong.

Statistics show that victims are at higher risk when they leave; many lose their lives. Not being able to witness his mood filled me with anxiety. The few times I would leave him, I became more frightened. Over the years, I learned how to predict his behavior. I was usually on point. I knew if the argument escalated from yelling and screaming into verbal abuse to eventually physical. Depending on whether alcohol was involved, I might be intimidated by a gun suddenly appearing on the nightstand or the kitchen counter. When I was not with him, I felt anxious and scared and returned home because I felt safe witnessing his behavior, as crazy as it sounds.

My anger was out of control, and I would release it through verbal attacks on him, hoping I could inflict pain. Words became a powerful and highly destructive weapon. Afterward, I was disgusted and hated the person I had become. As unhappy as I was, leaving was still not an option. At any given moment, the extensive list of excuses I was now a proud owner of was at my disposal. As the years went on, I continued to isolate myself, especially when there was proof after a fight and I could no longer hide the evidence. However, I discovered there is a form of shame I could hide with long sleeves and turtlenecks, despite the weather, and makeup works wonders depending on the shade of bruising. If we had plans and neither worked at hiding evidence, I could suddenly "fall ill" and cancel plans. If, for some reason, someone got a glimpse of a bruise, I quickly produced a story to cover it up. Physical scars are not always the ones that leave a mark. The ones that do are within. They are the ones that will surface in the next fight or with a simple act of disrespect. These scars manifested as anger; shortly after, I buried them again. I have asked myself countless times why I did not leave.

To this day, I cannot provide a justifiable answer for remaining in a toxic relationship as long as I did. Fear was a force that was always present, but by now, I must admit it was not the only reason that kept me from leaving. I became part of the problem, actively destroying my life. I found myself trapped in the cycle of the chain of emotions, each with a solid link to the next. God wanted to help me escape the emotional prison that had been my dwelling place for many years. When we lose our sense of worth, the scariest thing is that we no longer believe we deserve better and settle. The Lord reminded me I am worthy of love and respect. The revelation of how closely related fear and anger are was crucial to addressing the guilt, shame, and regret I have carried for years. The fear introduced through a violent act, especially from a loved one, will leave anyone hopeless. This phrase helped me understand I needed to forgive myself for how I reacted because there was no way of knowing how to respond and deal with such a traumatic event.

After many years of going back and forth, I was finally living alone; it still felt like he was somehow controlling me from afar. I developed a ritual I practiced for months; every time I would come home, I checked all the closets and bathrooms to ensure I was alone. It became an obsessive habit. I opted just this year to stop taking part in that ritual. Simply making this small change was not easy. It has taken a while, but I am slowly taking control back. I chose to free myself. I am learning to trust God with all my being, but there are still moments when I get an unexpected visit, and I run into that fear. It shows up late at night, like an old loyal friend preventing me from falling asleep. It could be a memory that comes to mind, triggered by a familiar noise or experience, reminding me of an unpleasant moment. Sometimes, watching something on television, primarily if the news reports another senseless death related to domestic abuse, I am instantly transported to an unwelcome memory. Yet, in those very moments, I surrender to the Lord. I am eternally grateful for His protection. On a positive note, one thing has changed when fear appears: anger is no longer a companion. I will continue to pray until there is no trace of this fear. That day is closer than ever because the Lord has told me so. It is a matter of time; it begins with breaking old habits. I am grateful because I cannot be in better hands than those of my loving Savior. He always protected me and kept me safe. He never left me. The Lord knew I would return. It is the reason He graciously sent me this wonderful message, a reminder that He wants to set me free from the prison of fear, anger, guilt, shame, and regret, the emotions I knew all too well. This message is the perfect road map, leading to a place filled with peace and love.

Still, it was not easy, because the fear I had lived with began to take on a new form. I began to doubt I could make it alone. That is when I found a seed of faith and told myself that no matter how scary or great the pain would be, it was time to set myself free, begin healing, and find my purpose. Exhausted, I surrendered; I said, "Jesus, I am ready." He then placed His loving arms around me and reminded me of the special little girl I once knew, full of dreams, hope, and love. In the end, it does not matter how long I stayed because I now live in the Lord's peace, which surpasses all understanding.

Note to the Reader: Remember…You Are Courageous

When we struggle with guilt and shame over how we react to what happens to us, we acquire deep scars, which constantly remind us of the possibility that we should have done better. We must look beyond our imperfections and return to our wounds, or we will miss the lesson. We cannot allow those reactions to define us. Recognizing the link between fear and anger will help us rediscover the courage that God has given us. This change in perspective allows us to forgive ourselves and begin the journey toward healing. In this chapter, the Lord kindly reminds us that anger is a by-product of the fear that manifests from what we have been through, allowing us to understand our reactions better and move forward confidently and gracefully. Through God's unwavering love and support, we find the courage and strength we need to overcome all challenges that come our way.

CHAPTER 3

Faith

I want you to go to the top of the
mountain, and I will meet you there.

Show me the right path, O Lord; point out the road for me to follow. Lead me by your truth and teach me, for you are the God who saves me. All day long I put my hope in you.

—Psalm 25:4–5, NLT

Look up! These words come to mind when I need divine assistance. It has always been the direction I turn toward when I need God. This phrase confirms that I have been looking in the right direction. The instructions are to climb to the top of a mountain where I will meet with God Himself. It is the most important of invites I have ever received. Simply looking in the direction commonly associated with His dwelling place is no longer sufficient. He has a request; I must climb and reach the top. Knowing God is anticipating my arrival is extremely intimidating because I do not believe I have the faith required for the journey. Although I discovered His plan was perfect because, unbeknownst to me, He had already prepared me to take the first step. When I first came to Him, lost and with my sense of belonging revoked, the Lord reminded me that the most critical aspect of my identity is that I belong to the almighty God. He also helped me confront the fear that had been a lifelong companion by reminding me of the courage He placed within me. The numerous trials and challenges I have endured have made me aware of the profound difference between believing I have faith and knowing I do.

There is truth to the common expression, "Everything happens for a reason." My faith in God tells me there are also no coincidences in life. Whenever my path crosses with another person, it results in a blessing, a lesson, or both. As it turned out, on this day, I was on my way home from work and decided to stop at a home store. I had nothing specific to purchase. I was browsing up and down the aisles; I could spend hours shopping and become easily distracted by all the beautiful items. I then unexpectedly heard my name and saw Angelica.

Mutual friends had introduced us right before I moved from Douglas. Although we had only spoken a couple of times, we were overly excited to run into each other, as usual when you are far from home and come across someone you know. We were chatting away, obstructing access to actual shoppers; she asked me if I had time to join her for dinner. I gladly agreed, and the rest is history; from that day forward, we became inseparable. This chance encounter resulted in one of my biggest blessings. She is warm and kind. Truly one of the most remarkable people I have ever met. You know those people that make you feel important, loved, and as if you are their favorite person? Angelica possessed this gift, among the lengthy list I would later uncover. I am amazed at how the

Lord always takes care of our needs. How He moves the pieces of the puzzle is nothing short of a miracle. She later confessed she also believed God crossed our paths for a reason and that it was also a blessing for her. The Lord's plan brought us together at the perfect time. I did not know much about her, but I had heard she had health issues.

Shortly after we connected, I entered a new phase of my life. I found myself alone, unable to cope with losing my lifelong relationship. In contrast to what I was going through, she could not escape her constant companion. She had been dealing with its annoying presence for over twelve years. It was stubborn and highly persistent. Its name is cancer. God knew we each needed the physical presence of a friend. We both have many friends, but none lived in Tucson. She had her home in Douglas and would travel to Tucson for all her medical appointments. Due to the seriousness of her illness, you could say she practically lived here.

A few months after we connected, she rented an apartment, making it a more permanent residence. It allowed her to rest instead of driving back and forth. She and her husband were separated but got along well and remained close. Given our circumstances, we were available for one another at any moment. It had been a few years since receiving my message. I was about to understand the meaning of this phrase because I discovered she had been climbing her mountain for quite a while. Perhaps it was why we crossed paths; she would teach me the definition of perseverance.

I began counseling with a therapist in Mexico, and I shared with her that I received a note from God a few years back during one of my appointments and that He had recently revealed I was to write a book using the message He sent me. I explained to her that it consists of seven phrases, and phrase number three is the one that has me perplexed. She looked at me as if I had lost my mind. After I read them to her, she seemed surprised. I was eager to hear her thoughts. I told her, "I have no doubt when it is time, He will reveal its meaning, as He has with the first two phrases." She then asked if she could share what she thought the phrase meant. I said, "Yes, please do!" She said, "Obviously, reaching the top of the mountain requires a climb. I believe you started your climb the moment you chose to get help. However, seeking help is just the beginning. You should know the climb will not be easy. But if you want to meet with God, you must persevere. All He represents is waiting for you once you reach the top." I was shocked because her description of the phrase resonated with me. At last, it was clear. I know the Lord enlightened her with the meaning of the phrase.

I do not recall ever needing God as much as I did at this point in my life. I had been reaching out, but all my attempts were unsuccessful. The frustration that I no longer felt Him close to me placed a greater distance, but I always knew He had not abandoned me. After a period of much-needed reflection, it was clear that denial and pride were a couple of barriers blocking our connection. I had no intent to perform an internal inventory of my bad choices and actions, anticipating the guilt and shame that would follow, but it was time. It was easy and safe to remain the victim instead of seeing the awful person I became. I used to blame others. Then, I realized that this was only a short-term solution. It was not until I reached rock bottom that I realized I paid a high price trying to avoid accountability. Losing myself in the process was not worth the temporary relief of shifting the blame.

While witnessing Angelica face challenging obstacles, I realized that I, too, would encounter struggles on this journey. Despite her treatments' painful side effects and uncertainty, she persevered and never gave up. Even when she received news that her condition was not improving, she continued to climb toward her goal. Since finding myself in a dark and hopeless place, I realized that the only way out was to start climbing. There was no better time to look up and begin my ascent. Faith is crucial, but I knew I needed to prepare before starting this journey.

However, God did not point out which mountain, nor were there instructions regarding my climb, which initially had me believe I would search for an actual mountain. I have never been outdoorsy, so when I first read this phrase, it spiked my curiosity. In case I was to climb physically, I researched the subject of mountain climbing. Before this, I had no idea it was considered an extreme sport; one site described it as

"The ultimate challenge of strength, endurance, and sacrifice." The description alone is intimidating. Mountaineers need to prepare mentally and physically, and they must also consider several aspects before initiating the climb. The altitude, the terrain, the weather, and the appropriate gear are just a few on the lengthy list. Even though my climb was symbolic, preparation was critical because my goal was to reach my destination. There are many similarities between climbing a mountain and my life. The highs and lows are the peaks and valleys. Each step can reveal the instability of the terrain during the climb, as with the events I encountered in my life. Each decision I made was as unpredictable as each step taken while climbing, and there was no way to predict the outcome. Some decisions I made with doubt proved to be wise, while others made with confidence did not always result as expected and brought unimaginable consequences.

Most of us know that mountains are of great significance in the Bible. Many stories take place on top of a mountain. God used them as the setting to meet with those He called. He planned to transform their lives. All these men had a common desire to connect with God. The invitation provided them with the opportunity since it would take them into His presence. Despite the intimidation and uncertainty, they obeyed and began climbing. Even though each man received a different message, they all had to conquer their mountain. Sacrifices, revelations, instructions, and healing awaited them at the mountaintop. I expect my invitation will provide the same outcome. As it turns out, the mountain represents all the obstacles interfering with my connection with God.

God has a plan, and everything happens according to His schedule. Many of us attempt to control our surroundings to avoid uncertainty. I have always had a distorted idea of comfort, which allowed me to settle, eliminating discomfort as an option. I mistakenly thought this was proof I had faith because I refused to give up. I have two options: to continue to live in fear or surrender to God. I recalled the young girl who believed that God was guiding her. This memory inspired me to let go of fear and take charge of my path. Every obstacle we face is unique, and we all manage adversity differently. In this moment, I remembered God gave me the will and strength to choose how and when to overcome challenges.

By the time I met Angelica, she had mastered the art of perseverance because of her strong faith. After her diagnosis, it was a constant fight to survive. She was familiar with and knew how unpredictable and difficult her climb was. During her battle, whenever she received positive news, she was confident she was going to beat the disease. However, just as it was in the war against this monster called cancer, one day, she received a phone call that would set her back from the progress made. We met for dinner that night; the cancer had spread. She sat before me with her beautiful smile, still hopeful. She said she was ready to begin more aggressive rounds of chemotherapy. She believed this treatment was "the one" that would give her the miracle she prayed for and was hoping to receive. One of her secret weapons was humor. I know the power of a positive mindset when facing a battle with cancer is a must, and I have often read that laughter provides healing. I am not sure about that, but at least for a moment, it helps everyone forget about the seriousness of the illness, and everything seems normal. My mom was diagnosed with breast cancer; she survived both rounds with her opponent. These two women exemplify how faith, a positive attitude, laughter, and a smile are the best armor.

As for me, I had no more excuses. It was time to come clean sort of speak. It was easy to victimize myself, especially since I wore the evidence and had the scars to prove I was hurt and broken; however, there was more to the story. Not only did I know what took place behind closed doors, but more importantly, so did God. Knowing this made it challenging to attempt and withhold my participation. I am writing parts of this chapter for the second time. Initially, I had no intention of sharing all the details of my story since I was so ashamed. God kept working on me, asking me to disclose my whole story. Reassuring me that He does not just see my current state of brokenness; He has also witnessed the events I encountered along the road that brought me to where I am. Only He and I know the truth because he sees my heart and its entire contents.

For years, I used words as my weapon. And as the anger within me grew, so did its reach. I hurt my loved ones as they witnessed my transformation from living with fear and anger. I never intended to hurt anyone but could not deny I had. After all, being part of a toxic relationship where we lived many profound and life-altering experiences highly increased the odds. I was always aware of my ability to elevate arguments to dangerous levels. I know there are cases where the victim may not have projected their anger as I did, but this is my story and my truth. And sadly, I know it is true for many others, even though they will likely not admit it. I understood that to overcome the oppression of abuse, I must own my whole story. I became a victim through a cowardly and violent act. However, not long after, I shamefully turned my abuser into my victim. My preferred type was verbal abuse since I erroneously believed it was not as detrimental as the physical form I endured.

The truth is that denying or lying about my involvement does not erase my participation or the reality of living with the devastation of fear and anger. Unfortunately, we lived in a highly toxic and dangerous cycle for years. The only way to stop its destructive power is to take ownership of our actions individually. If I refuse to take responsibility for my wrongdoings, I delay confronting the problem, and the remnants will keep me tied to the past. At this point, I know that accountability is not optional. If I continue to avoid taking responsibility for my actions, I will forsake my God-given right to live peacefully.

I never addressed the trauma I suffered that fateful night. An event of that magnitude can impact someone's life in ways one can never imagine. At the time, I only wanted to forget about it and pretend it never happened, as did everyone else. Although we lived many years without another physical encounter, the damage was irreversible. I discovered and applied three steps that helped me prepare and climb my mountain; I refer to them as the gear I did not know I needed. When you find yourself at the bottom looking up, I hope you find value in these three steps, because if the outcome you expect is to be free from all that binds you, they must be applied. It took time for me to accept His invitation. But with complete transparency and honesty, I invited God to begin restoring me. When I took the first step, the true challenge began because the mountain's terrain consisted of confronting the pain, struggle, and obstacles I needed to overcome.

The first step is accountability. I needed to look beyond the misconception that accepting responsibility for my wrongdoings would excuse or delete the offenses committed against me. In reality, this is so far from the truth. Shifting the focus provided a veil to hide behind; this blurred self-image allowed me to remain a victim. I justified my aggression because the fact that I had to take responsibility remained obscured if I continued to pass the blame entirely. Undeniably, our environment shapes and influences our actions. At some point, I had to hold myself accountable for my involvement and how I reacted to what happened. Nothing can compare with the relief and freedom I will obtain once I stop hiding behind a half-truth version of my reality.

I paid a high price for not owning all my mistakes; it is the disconnection from God. An important thing to keep in mind is that there are no filters that can hide anything from God. I must own up to an extensive list of mistakes, and it is time for me to confess them. Honesty and transparency are crucial since they are the only way to connect with God.

At last, I began my conversation with the Lord and admitted the reasons I believed had led me to this point. Sifting through a lifetime of painful memories and owning my share of them helped alleviate the guilt and lightened the load as I started my climb. In this part of my process, I addressed the guilt and shame for hurting my loved ones. I have never liked the word "victim." I associated it with someone weak and defenseless. When I released the anger and rage, I no longer felt helpless, and this way of thinking continued to fuel that behavior. Mistreating him gave me a false sense of power and strength. I am physically weaker than him; using words to hurt him meant I was no longer the powerless, scared victim. I did not have to make a statement to adopt the victim mentality. I earned the title from the moment I blamed others for my current status. I placed greater emphasis on what I endured rather than what I did, deleting the possibility of admitting I was wrong. With this practice, all I accomplished was to delay my healing. Our journeys are unique, so the invitation to the top of the mountain is an invitation for one. God plans only to address the person standing before Him. He has been waiting. It is my opportunity to share, in my words, all I encountered along the road to my brokenness.

The second step is forgiveness. Taking responsibility made me feel worse; I felt more guilt, shame, and regret. None of us deserve to be disrespected, mistreated, or abused, but knowing this did not lessen my pain for hurting my loved ones. After all, this was the family God had given me. I am unsure I fully comprehend what loving oneself means because it sounds selfish whenever I hear it. When I have been hurt or offended by people I care about, I can eventually extend forgiveness because of the love I feel toward them. That might be why forgiving myself was nearly impossible. Self-love was nonexistent at this point; on the contrary, I disliked the person I had become. I blamed myself for allowing someone to abuse me, and for becoming an abuser. For being scared to walk away. For not controlling my anger. For betraying myself. The reality is that when others shared their unfounded opinions and passed judgment, all I did was focus on my shortcomings and transgressions. Forgiving myself seemed almost impossible.

Since I had not healed, the projection of my intentions remained distorted. Learning to dismiss the unfounded, judgmental comments was helpful; I had to remind myself that no one walked in my shoes. Maybe if they had, their reactions would be the same as mine. I realized I had to forgive myself for how I engaged with two people in my life: my father and my partner. I went back to connect with the young girl who longed to be loved by her father, and then with the frightened young woman I was on the night of the fateful encounter; I comforted them for being scared and not knowing what to do at the time and for many years that followed. As a twenty-two-year-old new mother dealing with an addict who happened to be the man I loved, I had no skills or experience to handle an unexpected act of violence of that magnitude; I do not think anyone does. Yet, despite my immaturity and inexperience, I did what I believed was right. I did the best I could with what I knew at the time. Now that the story has unfolded, I know I should have handled things differently because of what I have learned, but I cannot change the past. I can only do better going forward. Even though I have made terrible mistakes and failed, God extended the invitation to meet with me, and His mercy has healed me. I learned that by forgiving myself, I am on the path to discovering self-love, a practice I will continue.

Finally, the last step is to surrender. God is the only one who can heal and restore me; from that moment forward, I surrendered unconditionally. He alone has the power not just to redeem but to take what is in pieces and make me whole again. Connecting to my faith allowed me to reach a higher level of understanding because I now know God is my loving, concerned, and caring Father. I returned to Him knowing He understands my struggle because He is a witness to my entire life. After applying these three steps, I have lightened my load, and I am no longer afraid to initiate my climb because I am confident I will conquer my mountain.

Our journeys are unique and specific to address the issues we have struggled with and must overcome. It is a miracle God equips us with all we need to succeed. Angelica remained focused on arriving at the top and meeting her Creator. She fought against a persistent opponent, determined to discourage her while climbing. Aside from her faith, she possessed grace and a larger-than-life heart with love for everyone. When we first connected, I knew that the odds were not in my favor because of her diagnosis and declining health, and I would eventually deal with her loss. I was not ready to add her to my already long list. Instead, I focused on enjoying the blessing I received when our paths crossed.

We made the most of our two years together; we laughed, cried, and ate at every restaurant she craved. We remained hopeful, even though it was impossible to ignore the changes. I will never forget the last time we saw each other; she had lost quite a bit of weight and no longer had an appetite. Long gone were the nights that began with the debate of where to eat and our never-ending conversations. This night was different. We held hands as we quietly snuggled on her sofa. We both knew the end was near. I could feel it. I asked her if she was scared, and she replied, "No, I am not scared; I am tired and ready." She said this as she smiled. I stared at her, containing my tears.

To say that during her climb, Angelica faced adversity is an understatement. However, her illness did not stop her from being in the present moment. She loved, lived, and enjoyed her life. Her positive attitude would not allow her to give up, no matter what. She remained focused on the path before her, overcoming every obstacle and grateful for every breath she had left. And I do not doubt that, as promised, the Lord awaited and welcomed her into His loving arms. To this day, I do not understand why loving, kind, caring, and generous people die. Based on my faith, I am referring to the physical end of our life. But I have learned to accept it because I know she dwells in the presence of God and is no longer suffering—the example of resilience and her warm and beautiful smile I carry with me in my heart. Pay attention as you climb your mountain; you may encounter an angel because Angelica proves that angels exist and walk among us.

As for my climb, I did not possess the courage or strength required to take the first step, but thankfully, I know the One who will carry me. The Lord is just a prayer away, waiting to help me. The journey to rebuild and find myself was unique. We will all face challenges, pain, and disappointment, react differently to what happens to us, and therefore end up in different conditions. Consequently, it is also not a "one size fits all" approach to healing. I no longer wanted to be my obstacle, so I took the first step in faith, knowing I was not alone, for the Lord was beside me. The times filled with doubt; He patiently waited for me to commit. When I feared and considered turning back, the Lord was my light, pointing out the path for me to follow. He carried me when I had no strength to continue and considered giving up. God plans not just to meet me but to support me along the way. He knew I would reach the top. My omniscient God anticipated all my needs and equipped me for my journey. I can tell you that it was not easy, and He never said it would be. All God asked was for me to accept His invitation. The process took time and brought more pain than I had experienced, but I kept my eyes on the prize; He is my reward.

Once I arrived, He was there, waiting for me as promised. Nothing is interfering between us anymore. God reminded me that with faith, everything is possible. Apart from receiving the invitation to meet with my Creator, what stands out from this beautiful phrase is that we all have a mountain to climb. Even though we may not be ready, the time will come when we must look up. Although some believe we will encounter several mountains in our lifetime, I am not sure I agree. Some challenges I faced, and will likely continue to experience, may appear mountain sized, but I believe it is the same mountain. Because I know now when I reach the top, I have conquered it for the time being, and it will not be the only time I have to overcome and persevere to remain in God's presence. Like any other relationship, it requires my commitment to seek Him daily and maintain the connection established. God gave me free will, and because of this, He then extended an invitation to meet with Him. He patiently awaited my arrival and handed me a gift wrapped with grace, unconditional love, and mercy; God calls it healing. Climbing a mountain is intimidating, but knowing it represents what stands between God and me encouraged me to take the first step. I am fortunate to be alive and humbled to have reached the top and been welcomed by none other than my Savior.

Note to the Reader: Remember…to Have Faith

When your time arrives to look up, do not hesitate and take the first step, even if you do not believe you possess the faith needed for your journey. Life comes with challenges and difficulties, which may seem more than we can bear. No one knows our pain, brokenness, or potential to overcome and succeed as the One who created us. The common question of "Where is God during bad times?" should be "Where do I stand in my relationship with God?" because He is always present and has never left us. It is us who have disconnected ourselves from Him. We stand on the sidelines, and we do not take action to help ourselves or others in need. God has given us free will to choose whether to stay still or move forward. If we continue to deflect responsibility and blame others for our reactions to our life events, we will remain disconnected from God. We cannot place the burden on God's apparent absence during difficult times. We must address what interferes with our connection and be accountable instead of blaming God and others for our actions and choices. It is the only way to successfully lighten our load and reach the top of the mountain. Go ahead and accept His invitation.

It is an invitation for one. During your journey, you will discover you already possess the courage and strength you need. When you are ready, take the first step; your compensation is to be in the presence of the almighty God.

CHAPTER 4

Promise

*You fear being abandoned; I will not
abandon you. I will never abandon you.*

The Lord himself goes before you and will be with you; He will never leave you nor forsake you. Do not be afraid; do not be discouraged.

—Deuteronomy 31:8, NIV

Many of us can relate to the fear of being alone; I have always been afraid of being or ending up alone. For my next chapter, there was a glimpse that God was preparing me to confront this fear. That is when I realized that I never noticed the lessons hidden in the seemingly insignificant daily events intended to teach me new perspectives. When my partner left, many things were challenging to address and overcome. The first one I became aware of was that our moments of bonding over coffee became a thing of the past. I used to look forward to the mornings because we enjoyed drinking coffee together. He likes to get a head start on the day and always wakes up early. It did not matter how early or cold it was or if I wanted to sleep in; he would always ask, "Are you getting up? Do I make enough coffee?" "Yes!" I replied and would immediately get out of bed to join him. It was our date almost every morning and the highlight of my day.

It was one of the rare times we had a conversation, with both of us participating instead of him just listening while I did all the talking. On these mornings, he was open and would share his plans for the day or what was on his mind. It was refreshing to see that he was more receptive and engaged during our chats over coffee. I never realized that hope was an added element besides the cream and sugar in those cups. It was a new day, with a calm start that began by connecting over coffee. There were no guarantees on how the rest of the day would turn out, but I hoped it would continue with the same tone. The morning after he left, I started the coffee and began to cry; in that instant, it was clear that those moments were gone, as was the dose of hope in every cup we once enjoyed together.

I realized it would be different now; it was then that I also became aware that I was now alone. At last, I would confront my biggest fear. It was not easy, and for months, I found myself crying, but one Saturday morning, as I sat in bed writing and having my coffee, I turned to admire a beautiful tree outside my window. I smiled and noticed I was no longer crying, and that is when I realized that the vital ingredient of hope was once again present in my cup. Without a doubt, I will encounter more challenges as I move forward on my own. Getting through this will take time, but for now, I am grateful a smile has replaced the tears as I enjoy my coffee alone.

I shared my coffee story with my sister, and she cried. A few months before, her close friend's husband unexpectedly passed away. She mentioned her friend also has a coffee story. Aside from the coffee, the similarity is that the dose of hope was no longer present in her cup. Looking back, I am thankful because finding myself alone allowed me to perceive God's presence like I never had. He reminded me that He is always with me; I now know I have never been alone. As for my sister's friend, when she least expects, she, too, will smile, for her cup will overflow with the beautiful ingredient of hope.

There have been many times when I have felt alone, lonely, or both. Sooner or later, we all learn the difference between the two. Being alone is a physical state while feeling lonely is emotional. It is unavoidable, and we all will find ourselves alone at different stages of life. It may be by choice or because of a life event, such as moving away to attend college or a job requiring us to relocate far from loved ones. Or it could be because of unexpected or unplanned events, such as a breakup, divorce, and death. And if you are like me, you may face one of your biggest fears when it happens. I have encountered a decent amount of loss throughout my life and have had to deal with the various emotions that followed.

During my childhood, I do not recall being alone much. I grew up living with my parents, grandfather, and three siblings; someone was always around. Even though concentrating on schoolwork or finding quiet time was challenging, I found comfort in the noise and chaos. Through this process, I finally realized that the root of the fear of being alone originated when I was a child and was related to my father's absence. I have few memories with my father, who only came for brief and infrequent visits. However, I would have preferred if he had never visited, as his departures left me feeling abandoned and alone. He stopped coming as time passed, creating a void that filled me with insecurities and self-doubt.

The other day, I shared some content from the book with my parents. I took that opportunity to tell my stepdad how much I love him and how grateful I am for him. I wanted him to know that my emptiness had nothing to do with him. Instead, it relates to all children's innate desire to feel loved and protected by their parents. Although my stepdad has been a father to me, I often wondered why my biological father did not care to be a part of my life.

Nonetheless, I longed for a relationship with him and hoped he would change his mind. Living in the same city as my father made me feel bitter and angry. I never understood why he did not visit. I vowed that if I had children, they would have a relationship with their father. Fortunately, he is the loving and supportive father I wanted them to have. He is always there for them when they need him. My daughter, in particular, is close to her dad; she is a "daddy's girl." Their bond is strong; she knows he will always be there for her. Two factors influenced my decision to keep my family together: I wanted my kids to grow up with their father, and I was afraid of being alone. Witnessing the bond between my kids and their father is where I found comfort when our relationship fell apart.

My personality is a perfect balance between an extrovert and an introvert, but ironically, despite my fear of being alone, I have always preferred the latter. It must be because I do not feel pressured to meet anyone else's expectations when I am alone. However, I only like being alone for a short time—a few hours a day, no more than a couple of days, is enough. I begin to feel anxious and afraid whenever I am alone. I must admit that even when the whole family was together at home, amid the chaos, chores, noise, and my partner and kids pulling me in different directions, I often felt like I was the only one there. My partner traveled frequently for work, and although I lived a comfortable life and had everything I needed, I missed him. He was always a great provider; I also worked and would care for our children and everything at home while he was away. At first, we argued a lot about how much time he was spending away because, aside from being gone for work, he had many hobbies that demanded his attention. Ultimately, I had no choice, so I stopped complaining about his absence and adapted to the situation.

As a mother, I struggled to make time for myself while tending to a house and my children's needs. I never realized how lonely I was because I was constantly busy with their activities. Our home was always open to their friends; I welcomed everyone and enjoyed having a full house. It gave me an excuse to cook and bake, which I love. Caring for my kids was the distraction that kept the loneliness at bay. I began to sense the void once they grew up and became independent, and their friends and activities demanded their time. I know that we all have limited time in this world and in the lives of others. And as much as I tried to prepare for when the day arrived that our children would leave home, it was still challenging. After they moved away, I was not just alone; I felt lonely. The size of the house and the quiet and empty bedrooms did not help. I focused on finding ways to stay busy; I always enjoyed and loved spending time at home, working on different projects and the usual homemaker chores.

We were blessed to have many friends and family who lived nearby. Someone always stopped by for a visit. It was comforting since I always preferred the noise and never welcomed or got used to the silence. My vision for when I got to this point in my life was to enjoy time as empty nesters before welcoming grandchildren. The reality was a lot different. After they left home, I felt lonely as my partner continued his frequent travel arrangements. As unhappy as I was with my life and could see our inevitable separation, I was not ready to face the fear of being alone.

As always, God's timing is perfect. Even though we may not be ready, it will happen on His clock. Our situation would get even worse. Shortly after the kids moved, he moved into our daughter's bedroom. I vividly recall that every night when he was ready to retire for the day, I would trace his steps walking toward that bedroom, followed by the sound of him closing and locking the door. It is a sound I have never forgotten; I believe that is what abandonment and rejection sound like. It was exceedingly painful, and that is when the fear I had as a child of ending up alone was more present.

My partner's distance brought back my belief that I was not good enough, the same feeling introduced to me by my father. By now, I was convinced I did not deserve better and continued to settle. It was just a matter of time before we parted ways. As lonely, sad, and unhappy as I was, I still could not let go; the fear of ending up alone was greater. Whenever I encountered people who were alone, I used to think they were not alone by choice but found themselves in that state for reasons beyond their control. I know now this is not always the case. Some people choose to be alone. I have discovered that having no attachment to anything or anyone is where our true power lies. There is a sense of freedom and empowerment that comes from surviving alone.

Unbeknownst to me, God's plan to address this fear was to isolate me even more, as it would be His way of introducing me to the most meaningful connection, the one with Him. The night I came home and found out my partner had left, I experienced something I never had before: a sigh of relief. In that instant, I decided I needed to take a different approach if I expected a different result. I reached out to family and friends in the past, but despite how much they cared and wanted to help me, they could only provide temporary relief. The noise in my

life provided a false sense of comfort, making me think everything was fine. And once I adopted this belief, it was impossible to connect with God. The purpose of isolation is to have no
distractions; it is the only way to experience transformation.
I have often heard desperate times call for drastic measures,
which is what I did. My survival and well-being depended on
the decisions I would make moving forward. I began by blocking and deleting people from my phone and my life. Some
would be temporary, while others would never occupy a place
again. God needed me to remove the crutches I used to get by.

To confront my fear, the obstacles and distractions that
held me back could no longer exist in my life. The Lord pos-
sesses the ability to hear my cries despite the noise. For me, the
noise made it impossible to listen to His voice. The key was to
silence the noise so I could hear Him providing much-needed
instruction. God removed everything and everyone that stood
in the way of our connection. I had to learn to be still and rely
solely on Him. There is reason and purpose in all life's seasons;
it was time to confront and overcome the fear. He was ready to
restore me as I sat alone in complete silence. In that place, far
from all that consumed my attention, with all the distractions
and priorities I had placed before Him no longer present, is
where my almighty God revealed Himself.

I have heard the story about the Potter and the clay. And
now, my time has come to visit the Potter's house. He awaits
my arrival. I am the clay He has chosen for His masterpiece;

He already has the vision for the finished product and a plan and purpose for the vessel. There is no time to waste; He begins cleansing by sifting and removing the impurities. It is where He will address my fears, insecurity, and everything hindering our connection. This part of the process is painful, but it is necessary. It was time to resurface old wounds that, over time, had become scars. Just because the scars are visible, and I may even remember how I got them, it does not translate to learning the lesson. One by one, God helped me address each one. He helped me dig deep and dissect them, and ensured that this time I did not just get by, but I aced the test.

Next, the Potter takes the lump of clay to the wheel and carefully begins forming it into the vessel fitting to His liking. This step takes time because the clay will resist taking shape. Like in my life, my stubbornness and disconnection only placed a greater distance between us. All I accomplished with my resistance was to delay my healing. The Potter is committed to His vision and returns the clay to the wheel as often as needed. He is engaged and molds it until He is satisfied with the vessel; He never gives up. After all, the Potter is a master of His craft. Once He is confident with the finished product, it is placed on a shelf to dry. This period is critical because the vessel will only be useful if allowed the proper time to dry completely.

During this time of isolation, when I felt abandoned by God, in those moments of complete silence, and when it appeared He had forgotten me, He had placed me on the shelf.

This waiting period helped strengthen my faith, and as a result, I overcame obstacles and learned from the challenges I have faced through the years. Once the vessel has dried, the Potter places the piece in the kiln for the firing process. The soft and delicate vessel has hardened; it is now solid and durable. God returned me to the fire. Initially, it appeared I would never survive. However, placing me back in the fire reminds me that the trials in my life are to give me strength, which is why I endured the heat. He tested me over and over until I passed. My commitment to the Lord during this time resulted in a solid and everlasting faith and relationship. As the Potter holds the finished product, he delights in His creation; His masterpiece is now ready for its purpose.

I am always in awe of God's grace. He waited for me to be still, then took each piece and put me back together, using His love as glue to make me whole. This experience helped me discover the incredible power of sitting alone with God. The word for this chapter is "promise" because this is what the phrase means to me—there are several synonyms for "promise," such as commitment, contract, and covenant. Sadly, most of us do not understand the true meaning or definition. I am blessed to know that from the moment God created me, He established a covenant between us, which means that through it all, He is beside me; I need not fear, for I am never alone. In Jeremiah 29:13 God says, "And you will seek Me, and you will find Me when you seek for Me with all your heart." God wants me to enter the next season transformed by this reminder, as He delivers me from years of living in fear of abandonment and rejection. The sense of disconnection from God was never because He had abandoned me; instead, it was because I expected others to provide answers and security when I should have been seeking only God. It is difficult to find a grain of positivity in certain situations, as it was for me when I lost my family and life as I knew it. Although some events will initially bring forth fear, the blessing lies in being alone despite the uncertainty because those moments solidified my faith.

Throughout history, there were times when God was silent, causing believers to question His provision and promises, but it was a test to increase their faith. I learned that I should never interpret God's silence as absence. His voice will prevail in this place of complete separation and isolation. I found my strength and courage, and it is because I know that in the darkest moments, in the midst of the crippling fear and pain, He was there. I finally understood He is my omnipresent God. He was by my side all these years, patiently waiting for me to be still. As I sit in this peaceful stillness, I can confidently say that I now hear His calming, reassuring, and loving voice. After I completed this chapter, this is one of my prayers: "Lord, thank you for silencing the echoes from the past, for allowing me to listen to your voice through the stillness of the present, and for giving me hope to look forward to the sweet sound of the future."

Note to the Reader: Remember…His Promise

It is safe to say that most of us believe there is a God or something greater than us. For me, it has been and will always be Jesus. Connecting with God does not require any complicated formula or ritual; it only requires making a choice. He sees our pain and hears our cries. Yet, to listen to His voice, we must silence the noise. In this place of complete stillness, we hear His voice and discover the God-given strength we never knew we had. When you arrive at the Potter's house, allow Him to mold you as the masterpiece He intended you to be. God plans to strip away all that hinders us from connecting with Him. In this process, He removes the obstacles that have crippled us in the past, and He patiently grants us the time to overcome all we have lived as He unveils the lessons from the challenges we have faced through the years. Your journey will be unique and specific to your state when you arrive. None of us go through the same things, react the same way, or end up in the same condition. But rest assured, the Potter knows what the finished product looks like; God has never lost sight of His vision for our lives or the purpose of His vessel. Once we remove all that impedes us from establishing the connection, we will experience an utterly incredible relationship with Him as He reminds us of His beautiful promise and reassures us that He has never abandoned us. Be still and know that He is God.

CHAPTER 5

Love

I AM *a just God.*

For God so loved the world that he gave his one and only Son, that whoever believes in him shall not perish but have eternal life.

—John 3:16, NIV

One of the verses in the Bible states, "You will know the truth, and the truth will set you free" (John 8:32). This means that to attain freedom, one must know God, who embodies truth. The term "knowing" refers to intimacy. Therefore, to be free from all my burdens, I must be willing to approach God in a vulnerable state, no longer attempting to cover my sins. There are many ways to be deceitful when telling my story, especially when shame is involved, and plenty of reasons exist to justify specific behavior. However, when I began to write this book, I realized that being transparent and taking ownership of my entire story was necessary. Though I was not prepared to reveal certain parts of my life, withholding them would only delay my healing and limit the impact my story could have on others. I have been held captive by my past and have been seeking freedom for far too long.

Throughout my life, I have faced numerous challenging experiences, and it is clear now that I should have practiced a different approach on several occasions, especially when the outcome was far from positive. When I used to hear "God is just" as part of a sermon, I perceived it as an attempt to persuade me to confess my transgressions without hesitation and fear, as if those three words were an incentive to seek God's forgiveness.

When I began this journey, I thought I would write a personal journal, and as soon as it was complete, I would burn or shred it since the last thing I expected was to expose the shameful parts of my life. I abandoned the idea because of the tremendous healing power I uncovered in the message. God wants me to share what I learned. I am motivated to comply because I have experienced significant growth and healing. After all, life is nothing more than an eternal classroom, where we benefit when others are willing to share the lessons from their experiences. It is challenging to share parts of my life because even the words themselves sound disgraceful; these words are *abuse* and *affair*. These are complex topics to talk about and write about because they contribute immensely to the shame I have lived with for a significant part of my life.

There are many experiences in my life where my participation was less than desirable, but they are easier to admit and more relatable than the ones that have brought on more shame. The entire message is a beautiful reminder that God plans to remove the weight from the fear, anger, guilt, shame, and regret I have been living with, which, sadly, many of us are familiar with for one reason or another. These emotions are powerful enough to interfere when I try to connect with Him. I am fully aware that prayer and communication strengthen our relationship with God. Lately, however, I have restricted what I am willing to admit regarding my mistakes. When I was young, I never hesitated to share with Him what was happening in my life. I was not intimidated; I was open and never withheld anything. The times I did because of fear of disappointing Him, knowing I had done something wrong, would eventually end with a confession. As an adult, when my choices and actions were more substantial, my openness with what I shared with Him came with reservations. The prayers became shorter and less frequent. I attribute it to my shame; it became an obstacle. Although unsuccessful, I put significant effort into diluting the power of my omnipresent God, who already knows everything about me.

The abuse became the first shame contributor. It required I disclose I lived with fear and anger, which filled me with guilt. Soon after came the shame, and regret for how I reacted. Understanding how they go hand in hand was monumental in this process because gaining insight was how I began to forgive myself. This newfound awareness helped me deal with the guilt from all the pain I caused by unleashing the built-up anger I had, which turned me into an abuser. Without God revealing how closely related fear and anger are, I would likely not have made the connection. The word for this chapter is *love.* There was never a moment I did not feel loved by God, but since I was young, I developed the belief that His love is conditional on my obedience and good behavior. And this reasoning prevented me from focusing on God's most important characteristic: He is love. It is at the core of His identity. He is the definition of the word, which is why He knows the raw and real version of me and accepts and loves me just the same.

Sadly, instead of acknowledging God is the only One who has the power to validate our existence, we have become consumed with and seek acceptance and approval from our peers. The problem is, we are all in the same state of denial of our reality, attempting to cover up our broken condition. We are deceived by a superficial method of approval that requires no accountability and therefore provides no redemption. We use excuses and blame others, then hide the shameful parts of our stories for fear of being judged because we would undoubtedly face the scrutiny of society.

In exchange, we live pretentious lives with carefully crafted appearances. Nowadays, with social media, our image is more valuable than our character. We often judge and condemn others by what they have experienced before we know who they are. We form opinions before anyone can speak, sometimes just by outward appearances. It validates the phrase "We judge a book by its cover." We are pressured and expected to fit "the mold" or society's ideals. If we fall short based on someone else's opinion or standards, the verdict is that we no longer deserve inclusion. And this puts more pressure on us to cover our sins and mistakes. We need to proceed with caution when believing we are better than those who, in our flawed opinion, display questionable behavior. We are all just one decision or circumstance away from sin, from ending up broke, possibly homeless, or in the worst-case scenario, behind bars losing our freedom and life. None of us are exempt from having our lives change in a split second. It is easy to be critical of others until we face a shameful experience or consequence of our choices or one of our loved ones. The only difference between those we ridicule and ourselves is that we are more successful at hiding our flawed lives.

Shame is an equal opportunity emotion, and we will become acquainted with it because of our flawed human nature. As far back as I can remember, I have believed there are two imaginary scales to measure the degree of fault and punishment for our sins and mistakes. Man has a scale, and the other one belongs to God. I do not know how fair man's scale is because, interestingly, those who believe they can judge also justify and excuse specific behavior to avoid accountability. There is an undeniable benefit when using man's scale to measure the degree of our sins or mistakes; its leniency allows variables to justify our "unacceptable behavior." It allows us to blame others and our circumstances in order to justify our actions. This scale is dangerous because it is enforced based on man's limited and inaccurate perceptions of our character. Because if we are honest, how often do we share the truth of our questionable participation in any given situation? Using this scale is a temporary solution; it only delays the conversation with our Creator.

In contrast, the benefit of using God's scale to measure the degree of our sins and mistakes is that He has access to the depth of our hearts. God sees clear and factual proof of my intentions, and without me saying a single word, He knows my true character, not my projection. I cannot hide anything; God is the only One who knows the real me. Thankfully, the only One with all the power to condemn practices mercy and grace. And while we have mastered the use of filters and tirelessly attempt to portray a state of perfection, we need to remember God sees through all filters. He knows every one of our flaws and loves us just the same. Perfection belongs to God alone; none of us come close. We must not forget Romans 3:23, "For we all have sinned and fall short of the glory of God."

And we arrived at the perfect segue to address my second shame contributor, my affair. Of the two, this one is more shameful to share. But I decided not to allow emotions to control me. Nonetheless, I want to exercise caution when writing about this topic because my human nature wants to justify my behavior. And because man's scale allows for manipulation, it is where my flesh can find temporary comfort. The spiritual scale is of more importance to me. Being this transparent when addressing this part of my life and exercising vulnerability is not easy, but it lifted the weight I have carried for many years.

Obeying the Lord's request to disclose my whole story is how I found the courage I live with today. At last, He has set me free. Over the years, I have had numerous conversations with family and friends, and they have shared their thoughts on whether or not this was an "affair." Generally, they tend to agree that I had plenty of reasons to justify my decision to move on. I do not entirely endorse their viewpoint. I came to terms with the fact that my relationship with my partner was beyond repair. Leaving my home was difficult, but I knew I had no other option since he was reluctant to move. I found myself at one of the lowest points in my life. It was then that I met someone unexpectedly. I am unsure if explaining my emotional state qualifies as an attempt to excuse my behavior. That is not my intention because I chose to enter this relation-ship. I assume complete responsibility, as I should. But I know emotions influence our choices, despite having and practicing a set of core values.

At the time, I was working at a bank when we met, and it was about five days after I was publicly humiliated while attending a wedding with my partner. That night, I discovered he was having an affair because the object of his infidelity was also in attendance. It may be shocking, based on the years of living in a toxic environment, but until this day, I had never experienced this level of humiliation. Unfortunately, finding out was not the only reason for the embarrassing episode. I was so ashamed when I decided to leave the wedding; several guests witnessed his aggressive behavior as I walked to my car. At that moment, I just wanted to be invisible. This occurrence would force my exit from our home; I did not know it then, but it was a blessing in disguise.

There is so much destructive power within the word "betrayal." Even if I had an ounce of confidence, love, or kindness toward myself, finding out about his unfaithfulness finally overdrew the account. It made me question everything about myself. I recall looking in the mirror that night and desperately trying to find something attractive or positive, but I could not. It was not just physical; I stared long and deep to see if I could find the woman I used to know, the one that had been hiding for so long. She was long gone; she had more sense than I, who had remained where I no longer belonged. All I saw was disappointment and failure staring back at me. His infidelity deleted what was left of the already vague memory of the young girl full of hope and excitement when he asked me to be his girlfriend. I believed then I had finally found a place where I belonged.

Every situation we experience is meant to teach us a lesson. However, the anger, pain, and disappointment I felt at that moment obscured my ability to understand anything. Thankfully, it did not take long to realize that the experience revealed a worse betrayal than the deception of the man I loved. It was the one I committed against myself, my betrayal. By far, this is the one that hurts the most. I lost precious years of my life and, worst of all, my identity. Ironically, the relationship I expected would fill my longing to belong would be where I lost sight of who I am. In hindsight, I am grateful for what happened that night; it was the storm that came to clear the path, leading me to find myself.

Through the years, I have met many remarkable people who unknowingly came into my life to add value; this man was among them. I know he came to remind me of what I had forgotten: I deserve love and respect. Of all my experiences, this one is at the top of the "bittersweet" category. I say this because this relationship positively impacted my life, despite the wrong timing. I always wished we would have met years later when I was ready—not knowing then that this encounter would set many things in motion. To say this relationship was unexpected is to put it lightly. I never believed I would fall into temptation, but it was hard not to because I felt like I mattered for the first time in a long time. I am aware of my flaws, and so is everyone around me. I have always considered myself an open book. What surprised me is that he noticed my qualities and focused on me, the person, not on my weaknesses and brokenness.

I recall the day I met him. It was one of those days when I was rushing, and nothing worked in my favor. My hair was not cooperating, and I had to get to work. Getting one last glimpse in the mirror before I left, I thought, "I look horrible!" But it was too late to try and fix my hair, and I left for work. Never could I have imagined that my life was about to change on this "bad hair day" as it did. It was late in the day; I was preoccupied and did not notice him standing at the service desk.

Oddly enough, there were no customers that evening; it was quiet. He was there because he had sent a wire to Europe, and his account was blocked. I proceeded to assist him with his concern. He disclosed that his family lived abroad, and the funds were for child support. After I resolved his issue, he showed me pictures of his two children, expressed how much he missed them, and mentioned he and his wife were going through a divorce. During our conversation, he spoke fondly of his family, it was obvious he missed them. He visited the branch frequently; my coworker/friend was his banker. We all eventually became good friends and began spending time together. It was nice to talk with someone who paid attention and showed interest in what I was sharing. He is a brilliant and noticeably confident man. It was difficult not to be attracted. There was a certain gentleness and kindness about him, and he was also in the process of finding himself given his current situation. He is an introvert and a bit mysterious, so I was surprised when he expressed interest in me. He disclosed he was attracted not long after we met. I told him all I could offer him was friendship because I was not ready for anything else, and he agreed.

We mostly had phone conversations and would speak every night. We discovered a type of intimacy that occurs when you connect deeply with someone's soul. I felt completely understood, accepted without judgment, and free to be myself. I experienced a new feeling; I felt safe in his presence, free from fear. For me, feeling safe was the best part of our relationship. But I constantly worried despite being careful and discreet; deep down, I knew we were both in danger, even though I was living on my own. I feared how my partner would react despite our separation and the fact he had moved on. For a few months, he did not pay attention to what I was doing; he was too distracted. As I anticipated, he was angry when he found out I was moving on, and I became concerned for our safety. I ended the relationship for several reasons—protecting him was the main one.

After it was over, I was perplexed. It was wrong, spiritually and morally, but it was too late not to consider the possibility of a loving and healthy relationship. It opened a window with a serene view where I could see myself living peacefully. For years, I felt terrible guilt. The spiritual struggle was unbearable. Upon reading this phrase, I knew the Lord had plans to address the abuse and my affair, the two primary sources responsible for keeping me enslaved. After engaging in that relationship, I was so ashamed. It is not easy to expose a connection that happened because I violated my moral code. But pretending and denying our feelings and experiences is unfair and no way to live. I want to hold myself accountable for my sins and mistakes. And also acknowledge and accept all positive emotions, like love, without shame.

If we could foresee and measure the devastation that occurs after an affair, most of us would likely abstain. My decision hurt many people; unfortunately, some still deal with the ripple effects. The cocktail mix of emotions is also something one never considers. I had moments when I looked for and found reasons to justify my affair to alleviate my guilt. At other times, I was remorseful, disappointed, and ashamed. Breaking my promise to God and my partner was painful. The result was a temporary disconnection from God and a permanent one from my partner.

When dealing with the demise of a relationship, we receive support from those around us while we try to put the pieces of our lives back together. We all have a unique way of looking at things. I have to say that I was not surprised when their remarks were in my favor since they believed I had reasonable cause to have had an affair. Unquestionably, man's scale was what they used to justify my actions. However, my primary focus is on restoring my relationship with God. I also had to process the pain I caused my partner. Revenge is a very destructive action, but truthfully, at least for me, it was not my motivation to enter that relationship.

Nevertheless, this logic does not excuse or lessen the pain caused by my decision. In hindsight, I wish I had been aware and able to assess the level of pain my decision would bring forth. But I failed to do so, and I cannot change it. After all, we only fix things after they break. It is part of life's process. From the beginning, I should have been honest with myself, left the relationship where I was no longer safe and happy, healed, and moved on. I am not saying this would avoid the pain I caused, but it might have been easier for others to accept my decision.

The phrase for this chapter instantly puts me at ease because, despite my flawed human nature, my almighty God understands me. Honesty and transparency are critical if the outcome expected is to be free from all that binds me. God is my faithful companion. He already knew everything about my life. He was waiting for me to begin our conversation. What encouraged me was to focus on the peace and freedom I would discover after taking responsibility for my actions instead of letting fear and shame deter me. Once the Lord forgave me, I was set free. The time to heal, let go, and move on was long overdue.

Nonetheless, each season of my life has an interesting way of teaching me a lesson. As a daughter, I had my share of issues with my parents. At times, I felt entitled to judge them for the mistakes they made. As life would have it, after becoming a mother, I had my share of challenges and struggles, which affected my judgment, aiding me in making poor decisions. I can see now how unfair it was to judge my parents. We are all victims of circumstance, of the environment we are born into, and we have no control over how it will affect us. Despite this, we are all just trying to do the best we can with what we know at the time. For me, it started with the pain and rejection introduced to me by my father's absence. I do not believe my father ever had any idea that his choices and actions had such a devasting effect on me. I know he never intended to hurt me; it just happened that way.

To this day, I struggle to accept that our children sat in our classroom and we, as their parents, failed to impart the proper lessons. Unfortunately, I do not get another opportunity to make things right. Our children were innocent bystanders. I focused on providing and exceeding all their physical needs but was clueless about caring for their emotional well-being. The dysfunction in our relationship introduced them to various emotions, primarily uncertainty and fear. Sadly, the version of me they probably remember is the angry and broken one I became after my first encounter with violence.

Both parents should share the responsibility for their contribution to the unhealthy environment. But for now, it is my turn to share my side of the story. I will never attempt to dilute or excuse how my decisions hurt them. I take complete responsibility. I pray that one day they can remove me from my role as their mother, not to justify my actions but to acknowledge my flawed human nature. And, finally, understand and forgive me, as I could forgive my father. I am committed to recognizing and addressing the parts that still need work and continually strive to improve myself. God knows there is always room for that. But I know I am loving and compassionate despite my room for error. This I know because the Lord has kindly reminded me. My greatest blessings are my children and grandson. And although I cannot erase their pain or resentment, I can pass the blessing of this message unto them and hope they connect with the Lord and heal as I have. God's plan is to heal and restore us all.

Knowing God always addresses me with love has allowed me to treat myself compassionately. After all, nobody knows better than my Savior that I am a collection of broken pieces connected to different people and experiences. Practicing accountability has been instrumental in my growth and new perspective. In my younger years, I viewed God as a judge waiting to convict me, but now I understand He is loving, merciful, and just. He knew I would face temptation, trials, hardships, and failures, leaving me filled with guilt, shame, and regret. However, God's infinite love and eternal mercy demonstrate that He can only be fair to His children. He showed me compassion without judgment and reminded me that His grace had already saved me. Writing this chapter has given me a deeper understanding of His love, and I am forever grateful because I know I am redeemed. He says, "Come to me; I love you as you are." This phrase reminds me that His mercy never expires, and I cannot do anything to lose His love. And I rest, knowing that He is always a just God, now and forever.

Note to the Reader: Remember…you are loved.

Appearance has become a word that consumes us. We place great effort in creating a different image from who we are to impress others. We tirelessly strive to achieve the picture of perfection and success; in exchange, we forsake our peace and even our happiness. All this effort might make us more enviable, desirable, and even likable by society's standards, but that is all. We use band-aids to cover our wounds and filters to create a better portrait to impress family, friends, and strangers who are unaware we exist. In our desperate search for attention and approval, we give up our power when we allow comments from flawed individuals like us to convict us. We live a pretend life. Which is just another way to say we live a lie. All of us make choices we are not proud of and have lived experiences that have changed us and filled us with shame. We hide them because if they are exposed, we become the target of judgment and ridicule. We walk around filled with ill emotions that convince us we are not worthy of God's mercy and forgiveness. And in our attempt to hide or deny our reality, we become enslaved. The truth is we seek acceptance and approval, and in this quest, we pursue our erroneous definition of success.

Eventually, we realize we pay a high price for temporary comfort and meaningless rewards.

Perhaps we should ask ourselves if we should be concerned with impressing those wearing masks to hide their pain and insecurities or shift our focus to our Creator, who calls us to come before Him naked, finally exposed, no longer blaming others for our sins and mistakes. God rejoices when we arrive as the mess we genuinely are. We can never impress God, not with what we possess nor by pretending to be someone far from who we are. The scripture says, "The truth shall set you free." An essential step to discovering the form of success worth pursuing occurs when we look within and stop blaming others for our current status. When we assume responsibility for our actions, shame is a thing of the past. The phrase for this chapter is an invitation to present ourselves as we are. It reminds us that redemption is part of God's plan because we are more than our mistakes, failures, and sins. He is saying, "Stop trying so hard. I know who you are, and I see your pain. Remember, I AM a just God. I understand, and I love you because I AM love."

CHAPTER 6

Hope

*I will guide you and deliver you from
the past—you must trust me.*

*For I know the plans I have for you, declares
the Lord, plans to prosper you and not to harm
you, plans to give you hope and a future.*

—Jeremiah 29:11, NIV

I have been alive long enough to know that loss is a normal part of life, but knowing I would inevitably encounter loss did not prepare me to deal with the pain, suffering, and void it brings. It was challenging to learn to live without the people and things that were once a part of my life; I struggled to accept my new reality. I remained tied to the past. I have uncovered an emotion responsible for this: that emotion is regret. It lingers long after a person is gone and the ink has dried on a divorce decree. Regret is the anchor to the past, even after healing has paved a new path. Throughout my journey, there was an essential step responsible for getting me to where I am today, and it required me to revisit my past. This process forced me to dissect every experience and learn the necessary lessons. Although I have gained extensive knowledge regarding where I acquired my emotions and finally understand why I reacted the way I did, I must apply my newfound perspective in this chapter. To say my journey has transformed me is an understatement. Since I have been on my own, I have reached several milestones. I feel different and know I am different; I have made progress. However, I cannot move forward.

Undoubtedly, the Lord has been with me, guiding my steps toward my purpose. He has reminded me that the most critical aspect of my identity is that I am a child of the almighty God. Through this reminder, God laid the foundation for healing. Next, He helped me understand the connection between fear and anger, allowing me to reclaim my strength and courage, which unknowingly were part of the gear I needed once I accepted His invitation to meet Him at the top of the mountain. As I climbed, the Lord strengthened and reinforced my faith. I did not know then, but faith is a prerequisite for the next chapter, where He planned to isolate me to help me discover the immense power one can find in being alone. I realized I was never alone; He was with me, providing comfort and hope. The Lord has been my constant companion. He is a witness to my entire life. He wants to remind me that I am understood, forgiven, and loved despite my sinful nature. I know God's love is sincere and pure. However, even after all these beautiful and powerful reminders, I am still stuck, afraid to move forward.

I always questioned why the phrase for this chapter is toward the end. I was confused because I had now traveled far from where I began and believed I had healed. But just like in previous chapters, God reveals the reason and meaning for each phrase at the precise time. It now makes perfect sense why it is toward the end of the book. Despite all the growth and progress acquired, as I learned to let go of the past, I still need to discover how to move forward. Letting go and moving forward are two-word statements that are overused and, quite frankly, underestimated. The commitment and discipline required to put them into practice go beyond the simplicity implied by reading them.

Several anchors are keeping me tied to the past, but the one that has had the most impact on my life was the relationship with my father, or, should I say, the lack thereof. He passed away on December 30, 2009, just after turning fifty-nine. When I was young, I would say, "If he dies before I do, I will not attend his services." This thought process was because I believed I did not owe him anything since he had never been there for me.

Several years ago, my family and I attended a church service where the message was about forgiveness. The pastor said that forgiveness heals and delivers us from the resentment, anger, and even hate we may have been carrying. He added that many times those we need to forgive have moved on with their lives while we are stuck living with these emotions that rob us of our peace. Until that day, I never considered myself carrying a heavy load filled with those ill feelings. For way too many years, I was angry and full of resentment toward my father, and he was not even aware, nor did he appear to care. I decided it was time to forgive him and committed to letting go of all that weighed me down. It is never too late to practice forgiveness and receive closure because I am relieved that God's mercy never expires regarding my redemption.

I was in disbelief the morning my sister called and told me that one of our brothers had gone to inform her that our father had just passed from a massive heart attack. In Mexico, the burial is the next day; they have the viewing the same night the person dies. As I was getting ready, I felt numb and over-whelmed with feelings I had never anticipated. Once I arrived, I felt awkward and out of place. There were many family members and friends, most of whom I did not know. They had an open casket. I felt deeply sad when I saw him; I could not hold back my tears. The first thing that came to mind was that I never told him I had forgiven him. And what was worse, I never extended an apology. My entire life, every opportunity I had, I expressed my anger at him for being a lousy and ab-sent father. I used sarcastic remarks not to sound mean, rude, or disrespectful. Standing before his coffin, I could not help recalling the last time I saw him; it had been about three years.

By then, I had already forgiven him, or so I thought. I ran into my father and one of my brothers at a supermarket. We had a pleasant conversation. Suddenly, I caught him staring at me; he smiled and reached over to hug me. There was a warmth in how he looked at me that day; I have never forgotten. For the first time, I thought he loved me and was even proud of me. For a moment, I hoped that he regretted not being part of my life and could compensate for the lost time. He never said a word. It was just me, thinking it may have crossed his mind. I only saw him a handful of times after forgiving him, so those encounters were pleasant. The next day I went alone to the service. My partner and the kids did not join me, and as I sat alone, I felt like a stranger, perhaps because that was what my father had been to me. I thought how ironic that everyone there knew my father more than I did, which is why I was surprised by my overwhelming sadness.

Before the burial, they had a Catholic mass on New Year's Eve. Over the years, I heard stories about my father's charisma and how he instantly connected with everyone he met, not just the ladies. Everyone stated he was a great and loyal friend. Wherever he went, there was always a crowd around him. While he was alive, I never witnessed that side of him. But on his last day here on earth, all those stories proved true. I was so surprised to see the church filled beyond capacity. Many attendees stood for the entire service; not the weather nor the fact that it was a holiday kept his family and friends from paying their last respects. I would have loved to have known my father as his friends and the rest of the family did.

When we arrived at the cemetery, they opened the casket one last time so we could all say goodbye. When it was my turn, I leaned over and whispered, "I will never forgive you for robbing me of the experience of knowing how it must feel to be loved and raised by my father and for always being a stranger to me." I could not believe I had said those things to him. It must be from the disappointment and pain because I never got to experience the warmth and protection a child should feel in their father's arms; now, it was too late. I gave my father a final kiss, one of the many I had saved for him, a kiss I hoped he would have loved to receive from his little girl.

As I stepped away, I asked myself, had I not forgiven him? I discovered the answer to this question was no. I still needed to learn the definition and requirements when extending forgiveness. There is more involved in achieving forgiveness than I initially believed. It consists of two parts. First, I must forgive the person who offended and hurt me; this part addresses the resentment and anger, emotions I knew all too well. And this, as most of us know, many times, is not easy. After this, the second part is to forgive myself for my behavior. I was disrespectful, rude, and, at times, mean toward him. It took me years after my father's passing to realize that I acquired all the ill emotions because of his absence, and this became an impediment to understanding him, his life, and his reasons for making choices that hurt me. I never had any empathy toward him; how could I? Investing myself in understanding my father was crucial in connecting with his pain. At last, I would discover the compassion I had never felt for him or myself.

An essential attribute of God's ability to extend everlasting forgiveness, aside from His undying unconditional love and grace, is that God begins by understanding and connecting with us. Therefore, He rules from a place of compassion toward His children. When I came to the Lord, pleading for forgiveness, His focus was on the daughter, who needed His love and mercy. Even though I traveled far from home, He ignored my flaws, mistakes, and sin and welcomed me with open arms, just like the father and prodigal son parable. God celebrated my return instead of pointing out the pain and disappointment I caused Him.

At last, I am holding the key that I have been missing all these years. I never tried to relate to my father in the only way possible: as a flawed and broken human being, just like me. I judged my father and struggled to forgive him. But God reminded me that I need to focus on his human side. After all, it is what we all have in common and how we are connected. God opened my eyes and emphasized that practicing empathy is how we can extend compassion. Once this occurred, I was able to forgive others genuinely. This practice is beneficial for me as well. I used to believe I was not worthy of forgiveness, but I never lost hope that those I hurt would try to understand what I had been through. We all play distinct roles in our lifetime. Separating the person from their role is crucial because it is the only way to acquire much-needed compassion.

I finally saw my father as a human with his share of insecurities and searching for love and approval, just as I was. After years of judging him, I could relate to him for the first time. There is one thing I knew about his life but had forgotten; his father had also abandoned him. It was strange, but I had never made the connection we shared with the absence of a parent until this day. The difference is that he was older when his father left. From what I heard, it was a morning like any other; my grandma made breakfast, and he left for work and never returned. No one ever saw or heard from him again. My father and his siblings had spent time looking for him, and they even hired someone to search for him, to no avail. Like I had questions about his absence, he undoubtedly questioned his father's abandonment. I had always wondered why my father was not interested in being a part of my life. The day I stared at him for the last time, lying in his coffin, I knew I would never have the answer, but now I know that how we each react to what we experience is not predictable or specific. Many factors influence our decisions at any given moment. Once I understood my father, I could relate to him and forgave him. At last, I am at peace.

Taking responsibility for my actions was easier than expected because of the comforting notion that God understands me. We are all shaped by the environment we grew up in. Despite our upbringing, we are all just trying to do our best. The pain and resentment introduced to me by my father's absence were the first things God addressed when I began this journey. I do not believe my father ever had any idea that his choices and actions had such a devasting effect on me. I know he never intended to hurt me; it just happened that way. Sadly, he died before either one of us issued an apology.

Unfortunately, there will be instances where we miss the opportunity to apologize or forgive someone, like in my case with my father. Even though I realized the importance of understanding someone else's experience after he passed away, I still found peace and closure. Only looking at things from my perspective prevents me from connecting with those who have suffered just as I have. It is impossible to know how someone will react to what they have been through, but we can try to relate to their experience. Understanding and compassion are essential for practicing kindness and creating a bridge to connect with others. It is the only way to start the healing process and move forward. Each of us has a unique journey, and many different factors shape our response to what happens to us. I find comfort in knowing that the grace of God applies to all of us because only He knows why things happen the way they do. I am grateful I have let go of the anger and resentment that robbed me of peace for many years. It is never too late to find closure.

As I mentioned earlier, regret is a powerful emotion that kept me from moving forward. And not in all the relationships that caused disappointment, anger, and pain would I need to practice compassion toward others. As I discovered, in many of my relationships, the person I needed to understand so that I could forgive was myself. I struggled with guilt and remorse because I hurt the people I love. And regarding the person who introduced me to the fear I have lived with most of my life, I would forgive him too quickly. My therapist might say I speak from my codependent state; she could be right since I am not a professional. Truthfully, at times, I cannot distinguish between my previous codependent tendencies and when I act with genuine love and compassion for people. I want to think that when I want to help others, it reflects my character and the kindness in my heart, enabling me to react with love and concern for the welfare of others.

One of my biggest regrets about living in a highly toxic relationship was that I got to the point where I consciously intended to inflict pain on the person who hurt me. I will never be able to recover either the awful words spoken, or the time lost. These days, knowing God did not waste any part of my experience and accepting that there is a reason for everything that happens to us are where I go to find peace.

In the past, I used words to hurt my loved ones. Despite this, God chose me to write this book. I am humbled and eternally grateful for the opportunity He gave me to reverse some of the damage I caused. This book is more than a collection of words; it is an opportunity to provide a glimpse into my journey, where I discovered the forgotten yet powerful meaning of redemption. I will undoubtedly continue to face trials and challenges and suffer my share of pain and disappointment. Still, God is reminding me that if I remain faithful, I can overcome, let go, and move forward. God wants to give me hope.

Amid all the chaos in my life, it was hard to remain hopeful. I used to be uncomfortable with change, but I was about to discover that not all change is bad. I was fortunate to experience the four weather-related seasons I learned about in school where I grew up. Although we missed the assortment of colors in the leaves as fall approached, I was still aware of what season it was. I found the rotation exciting. Depending on the season, I knew that even though there was discomfort from the cold or heat, it would not last forever, and the following season would provide relief regarding the weather patterns. I have read that seasons define our lives, and when everything around me began to shift, I found this true. I knew my life would never be the same.

Like seasons, we suddenly find ourselves entering the next one, whether ready or not. I was determined to prevent change; it scared me to lose what was familiar—even if it required me to sacrifice my well-being. As we approached the end of our relationship, I reached a point where it all finally felt different. I no longer had the slightest idea of what to do. But I did know that it was time to heal and find peace. I had grown tired of trying to prevent change from taking place. I was about to enter the fall season in my life.

The fall season has always been my least favorite. It is sad to see the trees lose their leaves abruptly, stripped of their beauty and robust presence. It appeared that from one day to the next, we went from the long, hot, sunny summer days with the plants thriving and beautifully displaying their colors to a drastic change. They now revealed a different and vulnerable appearance as they become exposed to unpredictable weather. There were no guarantees that in the coming spring, they would bloom again. We had a beautiful mesquite tree in our front yard. These trees thrive under intense sun and heat. The Arizona desert experiences severe weather patterns: it gets unexpectedly cold in the winter. Mesquite trees are hardy, and they can tolerate below-freezing temperatures.

One winter, we were reminded of the extreme weather we could experience. We had one of the coldest nights when temperatures dropped so low that they invited a thick blanket of snow. I worried about the plants, especially those I believed would not withstand the frigid temperature. I focused on a beautiful large palm tree, our landscape's focal point. That winter seemed determined to honor its name; it was one of the coldest I have experienced. I was anxious for spring to arrive to witness the lifeless, dormant landscape once again come to life. However, the mesquite tree took longer than usual to embrace the inviting spring weather. Sadly, it did not survive this winter freeze. It had to be cut, becoming firewood for the coming winter.

We never planted another tree. We talked about replacing it but had yet to do so. I was surprised the palm tree I did not expect to survive the harsh winter was once again thriving in its majestic fashion. A couple of years later, I noticed a palm tree was growing where the old mesquite tree used to be. It was odd; it had sprung up on its own. We intended to plant another mesquite tree but decided to leave it when we discovered it. Not long ago, I drove by what used to be our home, and I marveled when I saw the unplanned and uninvited palm tree had become as tall, strong, and beautiful as the original one. I parked and sat there admiring it, realizing the correlation with my life.

During my fall season, all I was focusing on was the change brought on by the immense loss that was taking place. I fixated on how my familiar landscape would be affected. I doubted I would survive the winter I was entering. In these dark and dormant moments, I did not consider the possibility of a different but equally beautiful landscape. My intent to prevent change obscured the possibility of remembering God is in complete control as soon as I surrender it. He had plans for my landscape; He set His eyes on the upcoming spring, where only what is hardy will survive. I surrendered and gave Him complete control of life's new design. It was challenging to let go and accept some people are not supposed to stay in my life for several reasons. Like the mesquite tree did not make it to the following spring, the same applies to certain people in my life. They would not make it to the next season.

As God began His work in me, the transformation was inevitable, just as it is when we enter each season. However, this time I looked through God's lens, He showed me what hope looks like in the midst of change and uncertainty, and I now see things with a new perspective. Fall has become my favorite season. As I look out the window, I hear the rustling sound of the wind, hinting that change is near. Subtle hints begin to appear, the leaves gathering and turning as they perform their last dance, the morning light a bit softer and more subdued as it gently enters through the cracks. The trees wrestle, attempting to hold on to their earthy-hued leaves, but the persistent wind wins the battle. The warm and generous shade they provided is now a thing of the past.

At last, surrendering to the cold winter ahead, the landscape appears lifeless for the next few months. Then, unexpectedly, the birds awakened by the warmth of the morning sun begin to announce in their synchronized melody we have once again survived another winter. And just like that, life reintroduces itself, and the landscape will soon thrive again. As it turns out, I was right; my life has forever changed. There is no way to prevent change or avoid the uncertainty brought on by the unexpected void it brings forth. I never imagined the impact it would have on my life. And although my landscape looks different and is constantly experiencing change, I welcome it. I am thankful God oversees the new design. He helped me focus on the upcoming spring. The Lord planned to revive and restore what He intended for good and replace what was lost.

Something new will always blossom and grow, unplanned or uninvited, just like that palm tree. It sprung up and filled the void left by its predecessor. God sees beyond what I can see, and since He created the patterns of the seasons, only He knows what lies ahead is far better than what I left behind. The Lord does not guarantee I will be free of the trials brought on by new challenges. However, He promises to remain faithfully by my side and ensure I make it through. As I trusted Him, I let go of what was and stepped forward toward a better way of life. I embraced my new season. I believe the phrase for this chapter reveals God's definition of hope, which, as it turns out, is the cure for regret.

Note to the Reader: Remember…to Have Hope

Many things in life are easier said than done. Remaining hopeful amid difficult and painful seasons is undoubtedly one that stands out to me. It is easy to be discouraged when we focus on the past because the only option is to accept what has happened. We cannot change the past and take back spoken words or actions that inflicted pain on those we love. Especially if the time to apologize may have expired, as it was for me with my father's passing. In such situations, regret appears, and we must find a way to make peace with that. When all is dark, the absence of hope is prevalent, and when we cannot see an end to our pain and suffering, we must remember to keep our eyes on the Lord, for He holds the answers we seek. We need to see life through God's lens. His eyes remain focused on the upcoming spring. Rest assured that He intends to give us hope in troubled times. However, we must be prepared for change, for it is, without a doubt, a part of His plan. When we finally surrender, we must never forget that we are in the hands of the most incredible artist. And as we marvel at our new landscape, although it will be different, it is also perfect and more beautiful than we could ever imagine. God's purpose for sending this powerful phrase reminds us that we will once again discover hope if we dare to look through His lens.

CHAPTER 7

Gratitude

Love others as I have loved you.

My command is this: Love each
other as I have loved you.

—John 15:12, NIV

When I first came across this phrase, I began to contemplate
the love of God. I have never questioned whether He loves
me, but I realized I had never thought about the way in which
He loves me. It has been almost five years since I started writing the book. It was challenging for me in many ways. I was
overwhelmed since I had no writing experience and believed
God had mistakenly sent me the message. Not to mention
that disclosing certain parts of my life was terrifying, shameful,
and something I never intended. The phrase for this chapter is
a biblical scripture, and I understood that God wants to em-
phasize its importance.

We often say that God's timing is perfect, and as I reach
the end of my journey, I could not agree more. He knew I
would return, pleading with Him to heal me. And, in each
chapter, the Lord answered my prayer, healing me without
judgment, reminding me that although I had traveled far from
home, He patiently awaited my return. I now understand that
God's love for me is unconditional and all-encompassing, even

when I fall short and make mistakes. He embraces me with all my flaws, brokenness, and shame. His love is visible, attainable, and never expires—it is eternal.

Before embarking on my unexpected journey, I applied the common practice of doing the asking during my prayers. Things shifted once I received my note from God. I began to pay closer attention and realized He also has requests. In this last phrase of His message, He asks me to love others as He loves me. Initially, I deemed it impossible because throughout my life, all I have practiced was the conditional form of love. I considered this a command and set out to find the answer. Despite the stories of God's wrath captured in the Bible, it is clear that His approach toward us, His children, derives from a place of love. No matter how we behave or act, God's love for us cannot be shaken or influenced by external factors. It is a pure and honest love given freely, without any conditions attached. I reflected on how God must have felt knowing I was on a self-destructive path. It was when I understood that the most significant proof of God's unconditional love was that He gave me life and set me free. All I received when I returned home was the warmth of His love. He welcomed me back into His presence—and healed me.

Throughout my life, I have hurt people I love, including my children. This has resulted in broken relationships that I have yet to mend. While being close to those I love would be ideal, I am taking a cue from God's approach and allowing them freedom while still loving them from a distance. I respect their decision and hope we can someday reconcile and establish a healthy connection. Forgiveness is a complex process, and we all apply different approaches. Some of us will desire to reestablish a relationship, while others may forgive and move on. I must respect and accept their choice. I pray that one day, they can find it in their hearts to forgive me, and we can make up for lost time. The seven phrases outlined in this book have helped me find happiness, gratitude, peace, and joy despite life's voids and missing puzzle pieces. The Lord has forgiven me. And it does not get any better than that. I surrender it all to God and know He will help me accept the outcome, whatever it might be.

Looking back on my life, I realize how much time I spent trying to prove a point, living offended, angry, and believing that others owed me something. Not being close to some of my loved ones has made me aware of how momentary life is, putting it all in perspective. These days, I try to live my life with fewer regrets. I practice gratitude and try not to waste any opportunity to spend time with those I love. I never miss a chance to tell them how much I love them and try to be kind. My ultimate goal is to leave a lasting positive impact on those who matter to me so they will remember me with a smile when I am gone.

Life is a precious and rare gift that we must cherish every day. It is like a storybook that unfolds with every passing moment, and time waits for no one. We should seize the moment, be present, and create as many memories as possible. I have met many remarkable people along my journey, and we have learned valuable lessons from each other. I cannot deny that my favorite person in the entire world is my grandson, Myles. There is something extraordinary in every child. As we journey through life, we lose our childhood innocence, but I firmly believe that we are closer to God during those formative years, which is why our purity is so unblemished. Myles unknowingly taught me the most valuable lesson: that we are born with the ability to love.

I went to visit my children and grandson in Phoenix. During our visits, Myles and I always engage in various activities, from playing games and snacking on his favorite treats to watching movies. Time spent with him is precious, and I am always eager to say yes. Reflecting on my parenting years, I regret not fully appreciating the value of time and creating more unforgettable moments with my children when they were young. I am determined to be present and enjoy every moment with him. I will do anything to make him happy and feel loved; these moments together are priceless.

We were home alone that night, and I washed dishes while he played with his toys in his room. He came running into the kitchen and asked if I wanted to color with him, which was his favorite activity. I gladly accepted, and we went to sit in the living room. It was heartwarming to see how excited he was about the little things. He pulled out his vast collection of crayons and coloring books and insisted on choosing which picture I would color. We sat beside each other and focused on our works of art. I watched him concentrate and carefully outline his favorite superhero. It was a precious moment. I was so happy to spend time with him.

Unexpectedly and without disrupting the dance that was taking place between his crayon and the paper, he said to me, "Nana, I love you, Nana."

And just like that, when I thought this moment could not get any better, I heard the sweetest voice say the most powerful words: this beautiful boy created the perfect moment. He touched me beyond words. I got emotional, and as I contained my tears, I asked him, "You do?"

He said, "Yes! I do."

The way he quickly and confidently answered my question made me wonder if he even understood what he had just said to me or the meaning of love, for that matter. Why did he want to tell me he loved me right then?

Curious, I asked, "How do you know you love me?"

And very matter of fact, he turned to me and said, "I don't know. I just do."

I thought his response was adorable. How he felt inspired to tell me he loved me was so thoughtful. I did not give it more thought. I stored this beautiful moment in my box of memories.

Writing about love can be challenging when one has not experienced unconditional love. At this point in my life, I am uncertain if I ever will. Yet knowing the Lord loves me this way is more than enough. I stared at my blank screen, unsure what to write. Then I remembered my conversation with Myles and arrived at this conclusion about love: that night, Myles was trying to say *thank you* instead of *I love you*. He was grateful I had put everything aside to spend time with him, but he could not express what he wanted to say. Instead, he said, "I love you." My grandson taught me that gratitude is a crucial component of love. And that love is the only emotion God has placed within us. The only way to connect with and express this gift called love is when we are genuinely grateful.

During my introspective journey, I delved deeply into my life experiences. And I have arrived at an eternal state of gratitude for the benefit and blessing of being a child of the almighty God. The best way to cultivate gratitude is by remembering the price Jesus paid on the cross. I am committed to loving others as God loves me. I will say that it is not easy, but what helps me is to look through God's lens. Although our beliefs differ, for me, God is the ultimate source and embodiment of love, and only in His presence can we genuinely comprehend its essence.

Arriving at the last chapter fills me with immense joy. Initially, I felt pressure to do justice to my story and make God proud. Despite my doubts, I persevered, allowing my imperfect and sinful nature to inspire me, which, as it turned out, was God's plan from the start. I obeyed his request and removed all the fig leaves, exposing all the areas He needed to heal. The Potter began working on His vessel until He was pleased. And with great pride, He unveiled His masterpiece, ready to fulfill its true purpose. This book contains an honest and unfiltered account of my life. The result is a deeper connection with my Savior. God has helped me understand who I am by revealing who He is.

Embarking on this journey has been my biggest life challenge but also the greatest blessing. Looking back, I have come a long way from believing life was no longer worth living. The night I told the Lord I no longer wanted to live, the Holy One appeared and sat beside me, the disgraceful sinner, just like the story in the Bible of the woman at the well who believed she was so far from God's reach and undeserving of love and forgiveness. I did not know what to call it that night, but I know now that God showed me grace and unconditional love despite my flawed human nature. He wanted me to know He had never abandoned me and was faithfully and unconditionally by my side.

I am eternally humbled and grateful that God invited me on this path of growth and self-discovery. Although I have come a long way, I am fully aware that I am still a work in progress, which is perfectly okay. Being mindful and present has enabled me to appreciate all God has done for me and continues to do. Ultimately, when I leave this world, all I will take with me is the overwhelming gratitude of knowing I have positively impacted someone else's life. I aspire to spend the rest of my life serving others because helping others is how I will fulfill my purpose.

And finally, I want to share my vision of heaven with you. I imagine a magnificent library with towering shelves filled with countless books. Each book contains the life journey of every one of God's children. These books are carefully recorded and preserved for eternity. In my mind's eye, I see the almighty Himself holding my book while seated on a throne of glory. I stand before Him with my head bowed, overwhelmed with emotion as He reads the pages filled with countless moments of joy, love, and gratitude, to name a few—as well as those that capture my sin, doubt, and shame. He sits attentively, reading my story, and with a gentle smile, the Lord turns to me, pulls me into a warm embrace, and says, "Well done, my beloved child. You have fulfilled your purpose. I welcome you into your eternal home." This image brings me a powerful sense of peace and hope. I know that in the end, all my struggles and achievements will be acknowledged and celebrated in the presence of my Creator. I used to believe my story did not have the fairytale ending I dreamed of. Yet the Lord has shown me that His definition of "happily ever after" is far better than mine. No matter what the future holds, it will never change the happy ending of my story because I discovered who the true and eternal love of my life is. His name is Jesus; He is my every-thing; I refer to Him as my one and all.

At the beginning of my journey, I was lost, convinced I did not belong and no longer had an identity. God unveiled the importance of understanding the core of my identity. When I recalled to whom I belonged, I found my new definition of success: I am a child of the almighty God and a work in prog-ress. We are all on a unique journey, and at some point, we must take control of the remaining chapters of our story. It is crucial to remember that God created us in His image; there-fore, we possess His capacity to love. Once we discover God's unconditional love, we arrive at an eternal state of gratitude. From here, our stories will end with a shared purpose—to love others as God loves us. Do not forget He is always beside you, whispering, "Remember... I AM With You.".

Note to the Reader: Remember…to Be Grateful

We cannot find love in grandiose displays. Instead, love is the sum of many small actions. We are here to fulfill the ultimate commandment to love one another as God loves us. Our duty as part of the human race is to uphold this purpose. We cannot survive on our own, no matter how much we may think we can. Looking at pictures of natural disasters and war-torn landscapes can be challenging. However, we must be mindful of our surroundings to fulfill our purpose. Aside from the devastation we can see in the images, we cannot deny that the best parts of humanity are on display, capturing the compassion we are capable of. During times of tragedy and suffering, the love that God placed within us is revealed, bringing us closer together. If we fail to reach this level of consciousness, we will have spent a lifetime not fully understanding the reason for our existence and the meaning of grace. I know it is not always easy to be grateful. A helpful reminder is to shift our focus to God and the cross, where it is clear that we are loved unconditionally despite our flawed condition. And this is a reason to be at peace and be thankful. I hope this message will inspire you to love others as God loves you.

Milton Keynes UK
Ingram Content Group UK Ltd.
UKHW020632210424
441310UK00007B/24